PYTHON

FOR

BEGINNERS

A crash course guide for machine learning and web
programming. Learn a computer language in easy steps
with coding exercises.

JASON TEST

TABLE OF CONTENTS

INTRODUCTION

Design patterns are reusable model for solving known and common problems in software architecture.

They are best described as templates for working with a specific normal situation. An architect can have a template for designing certain types of door frames, which he fit into many of his project, and a software engineer or software architect must know the templates for solving common programming tasks.

An excellent presentation of the design pattern should include:

- Name
- Motivating problem
- Decision
- Effects

Equivalent Problems

If you thought it was a rather vague concept, you would be right. For example, we could say that the following "pattern" solves all your problems:

- Gather and prepare the necessary data and other resources
- Make the necessary calculations and do the necessary work
- Make logs of what you do
- Free all resources
- ???
- Profit

This is an example of too abstract thinking. You cannot call it a template because it is not an excellent model to solve any problem, even though it is technically applicable to any of them (including cooking dinner).

On the other hand, you may have solutions that are too specific to be called a template. For example, you may wonder if QuickSort is a template to solve the sorting problem.

This is, of course, a common program problems, and QuickSort is a good solution for it. However, it can be applied to any sorting problem with virtually no change.

Once you have this in the library and you can call it, your only real job is to make somehow your object comparable, and you don't have to deal with its entity yourself to change it to fit your specific problem.

Equivalent problems lie somewhere between these concepts. These are different problems that are similar enough that you can apply the same model to them, but are different enough that this model is significantly customized to be applicable in each case.

Patterns that can be applied to these kinds of problems are what we can meaningfully call design patterns.

Why use design patterns?

You are probably familiar with some design patterns through code writing practice. Many good programmers end up gravitating towards them, not even being explicitly trained, or they simply take them from their seniors along the way.

The motivation to create, learn, and use design patterns has many meanings. This is a way to name complex abstract concepts to provide discussion and learning.

They make communication within the team faster because someone can simply use the template name instead of calling the board. They allow you to learn from the experiences of people who were before you, and not to reinvent the wheel, going through the whole crucible of gradually improving practices on your own (and constantly cringing from your old code).

Bad decisions that are usually made up because they seem logical at first glance are often called anti-patterns. For something to be rightly called an anti-pattern, it must be reinvented, and for the same problem, there must be a pattern that solves it better.

Despite the apparent usefulness in this practice, designing patterns are also useful for learning. They introduce you to many problems that you may not have considered and allow you to think about scenarios with which you may not have had hands-on experience.

They are mandatory for training for all, and they are an excellent learning resources for all aspiring architect and developing who may be at the beginning of their careers and who have no direct experience in dealing with the various problems that the industry provides.

Python Design Patterns

Traditionally, design models have been divided into three main categories: creative, structural, and behavioral. There are other categories, such as architectural patterns or concurrency patterns, but they are beyond the scope of this article.

There are also Python-specific design patterns that are created specifically around problems that the language structure itself provides, or that solve problems in unique ways that are only resolved due to the language structure.

Generating Patterns deal with creating classes or objects. They serve to abstract the specifics of classes, so that we are less dependent on their exact implementation, or that we do not have to deal with complex constructions whenever we need them, or that we provide some special properties of the instantiation. They are very useful for reducing dependency and controlling how the user interacts with our classes.

Structural patterns deal with assembling objects and classes into larger structures while keeping these structures flexible and efficient. They, as a rule, are really useful for improving the readability and maintainability of the code, ensuring the correct separation of functionality, encapsulation, and the presence of effective minimal interfaces between interdependent things.

Behavioral patterns deal with algorithms in general and the distribution of responsibility between interacting objects. For example, they are good practice when you may be tempted to implement a naive solution, such as busy waiting, or load your classes with unnecessary code for one specific purpose, which is not the core of their functionality.

Generative Patterns

- Factory
- Abstract factory
- Builder
- Prototype
- Singleton
- Object pool

Structural Patterns

- Adapter
- Bridge
- Composite
- Decorator
- Facade
- Flyweight
- Proxy

Behavioral patterns

- Chain of responsibility
- Command
- Iterator
- Mediator
- Memento
- Observer

- State
- Strategy
- Visitor

Python Specific Design Patterns

- Global object pattern
- Prebound method pattern
- Sentinel object pattern

Type Annotation in Python

First, let's answer the question: why do we need annotations in Python? In short, the answer will be this: to increase the information content of the source code and to be able to analyze it using specialized tools. One of the most popular, in this sense, is the control of variable types. Even though Python is a language with dynamic typing, sometimes there is a need for type control.

According to PEP 3107, there may be the following annotation use cases:

type checking:

- expansion of the IDE functionality in terms of providing information about the expected types of arguments and the type of return value for functions:
- overload of functions and work with generics:
- interaction with other languages:
- use in predicate logical functions:
- mapping of requests in databases:
- marshaling parameters in RPC (remote procedure call)

Using annotations in functions

In functions, we can annotate arguments and the return value.

It may look like this:

def repeater (s: str, n: int) -> str:

return s * n

An annotation for an argument is defined after the colon after its name:

argument_name: annotation

An annotation that determines the type of the value returned by the function is indicated after its name using the characters ->

def function_name () -> type

Annotations are not supported for lambda functions

Access to function annotations Access to the annotations

Used in the function can be obtained through the   annotations attribute, in which annotations are presented in the form of a dictionary, where the keys are attributes, and the values are annotations. The main value to returned by the function is stored in the record with the return key.

Contents of repeater .annotations :

{'n': int, 'return': str, 's': str}

4 programming languages to learn, even if you are a humanist

The digital age dictates its own rules. Now, knowledge of programming languages is moving from the category of "too highly specialized skill" to must have for a successful career. We have compiled for you the four most useful programming languages that will help you become a truly effective specialist.

1. Vba

If you constantly work in Excel and spend time on the same routine operations every day, you should consider automating them. Macros - queries in the VBA language built into Excel will help you with this. Having mastered macros, you can not only save time, but also free up time for more interesting tasks (for example, to write new macros). By the way, to automate some operations, learning VBA is not necessary - just record a few actions using the macro recorder, and you can repeat them from time to time. But it's better to learn this language: macro recordings will give you only limited functionality.

Despite its attractiveness, macros have two drawbacks. Firstly, since a macro automatically does all the actions that you would do with your hands, it seriously loads RAM (for example, if you have 50,000 lines in a document, your poor computer may not withstand macro attacks). The second - VBA as a programming language is not very intuitive, and it can be difficult for a beginner to learn it from scratch.

2. SQL

In order to combine data from different databases, you can use the formulas VPR and INDEX (SEARCH). But what if you have ten different databases with 50 columns of 10,000 rows each? Chances are good to make a mistake and spend too much time.

Therefore, it is better to use the Access program. Like VPR, it is designed to combine data from various databases, but it does it much faster. Access automates this function, as well as quickly filters information and allows you to work in a team. In addition to Access, there are other programs for working with databases (DBMS), in most of which you can work using a simple programming language - SQL (Structured Query Language). Knowledge of SQL is one of the basic requirements for business analysts along with knowledge of Excel, so we advise you to take a closer look if you want to work in this area.

3. R

R is a good alternative to VBA if you want to make data processing easier. How is he good? Firstly, unlike a fellow, it is really simple and understandable even for those who have never had anything to do with programming in their life. Secondly, R is designed to work with databases and has wide functionality: it can change the structure of a document, collect data from the Internet, process statistically different types of information, build graphs, create tag clouds, etc. To work with Excel files, you will have to download special libraries, but it is most convenient to save tables from Excel in csv format and work in them. By the way, it is R that the program was written with which we make TeamRoulette in our championships. Thanks to her, we manage to scatter people on teams in five minutes instead of two hours.

To learn how to work in R, first of all, download a visual and intuitive programming environment - RStudio .

4. Python

Python is an even more powerful and popular programming language (by the way, it really has nothing to do with python). Like R, Python has special libraries that work with Excel files, and it also knows how to collect information from the Internet (forget about manually driving data into tables!). You can write endlessly about Python, but if in a nutshell - it's a really convenient and quick tool that is worth mastering if you want to automate routine operations, develop your own algorithmic thinking and generally keep up with technical progress.

Unlike R, Python does not have one of the most convenient programming environments - here everyone is free to choose to taste. For example, we recommend IDLE, Jupyter Notebook, Spyder, for more advanced programmers - PyCharm.

You can learn how to program in Python and analyze data using it in our online course "Python. Data Analysis". The consultants from Big4 and Big3 will tell you how to work with libraries, create programs and algorithms for processing information.

Well, as it were, let's go

Well, if you (You, He, She, It, They) are reading this means we are starting our first Python lesson. Hooray (...) Today you will learn how to code. And what's more, you'll learn how to code in Python.

But to start coding you need Python. Where to get it?

Where to getPython?

But you think that now you can just sit down and cod. Well actually yes. BUT usually real hackers and programmers code in code editors. For working with Python We (I) recommend using a Jupyter Notebook or JupyterLab or Visual Studio Code. We (I) Will code in Visual Studio Code, but the other editors are no different.

Well, it's CODING time.

I'm too old for that

Everyone always writes the first code that displays "Hello World". Well, are we some kind of gifted? No, and therefore we will begin with this. In Python, the print () function is used to output text. To output "Hello World" we need to write the following:

It's alife

Yes, you just wrote your first program. Now you are a programmer (NO).

Let's look at the structure of the print function. This function consists of the name - print, and the place where we throw what this function should output. If you want to display any text, you need to write it in quotation mark, either in single or double.

But now let's enter some text. For this, Python has an input function. To accept something, you need to write the following:

```
1    a=input()
2    print(a)
```

What does this program do for us? First we introduce something, at the moment we don't care what it is, text or numbers. After, our program displays what you wrote.

But how to make sure that we write the text before entering something? Really simple. There are two ways to do this.

```
1    print('          )
2    a=input()
3    print(a)
```

How can, but not necessary

If you run the second program you will notice that you have to enter data in the same line in which the text is written.

```
1   a=input(         )
2   print(a)
```

How to do

But this is not aesthetically pleasing. We are here with you all the aesthetes. And so in order for you to enter values on a separate line, you can do the following:

```
1   a=input(          )
2   print(a)
```

Like cool, but why?

As we can see, \ n appeared at the end. This is a control character that indicates the passage to the next line. But it's too lazy for me to write it down every time, and therefore I prefer to type everything in the line where the text is written.

But where to apply it? Very simple, you can take math. There are some simple arithmetic operations in Python that I will tell you about now.

Python has the following arithmetic operations: addition, subtraction, multiplication, division, integer division, exponentiation, and the remainder of division. As everything is recorded, you can see below:

```
1   6+2
2   6-2
3   6*2
4   6/2
5   3//2
6   3**2
7   3%2
```

I will finally learn how to multiply

If you want to immediately print the result, then you just need to write an arithmetic operation in print:

```
1    print(6+2)
```

The result of this program will be 8

But how do we carry out operations with numbers that the user enters? We need to use input. But by default in Python, the values that input passes are a string. And most arithmetic operations cannot be performed on a line. In order for our program to work as we intended, we need to specify what type of value Python should use.

To do this, we use the int function:

```
1    a=int(input("          : "))
2    b=int(input("          : "))
3    print(a+b)
```

We add up the two numbers that the user enters. (Wow, I found out how much 2 + 2 will be)

1. PYTHON CODE OPTIMIZATION WITH CTYPES

Content:

Basic optimizations

Before rewriting the Python source code in C, consider the basic optimization methods in Python.

Built-in Data Structures

Python's built-in data structures, such as set and dict, are written in C. They work much faster than your own data structures composed as Python classes. Other data structures besides the standard set, dict, list, and tuple are described in the collections module documentation.

List expressions

Instead of adding items to the list using the standard method, use list expressions.

```
#Slow
    mapped = []
    for value in originallist:
    mapped.append (myfunc (value))

    # Faster
    mapped = [myfunc (value) in originallist]
```

ctypes

The ctypesmodule allows you to interact with C code from Python without using a module subprocessor another similar module to start other processes from the CLI.

There are only two parts: compiling C code to load in quality shared object and setting up data structures in Python code to map them to C types.

In this article, I will combine my Python code with LCS.c, which finds the longest subsequence in two-line lists. I want the following to work in Python:

```
list1 = ['My', 'name', 'is', 'Sam', 'Stevens', '!']
    list2 = ['My','name', 'is', 'Alex', 'Stevens', '.']

    common = lcs (list1, list2)

    print (common)
    # ['My', 'name', 'is', 'Stevens']
```

One problem is that this particular C function is the signature of a function that takes lists of strings as argument types and returns a type that does not have a fixed length. I solve this problem with a sequence structure containing pointers and lengths.

Compiling C code in Python

First, C source code (lcs.c) is compiled in lcs.soto load in Python.

```
gcc -c -Wall -Werror -fpic -O3 lcs.c -o lcs.o
    gcc -shared -o lcs.so lcs.o
```

- Wall will display all warnings:
- Werror will wrap all warnings in errors:
- fpic will generate position-independent instructions that you
  will need if you want to use this library in Python:
- O3 maximizes optimization:

And now we will begin to write Python code using the resulting shared
object file.

Structures in Python

Below are two data structures that are used in my C code.

```
struct sequence
    {
        char ** items:
        int length:
    }:

    struct cell
    {
      int index:
      int length:
      struct Cell * prev:
    }:
```

And here is the translation of these structures into Python.

```
import ctypes
   class SEQUENCE (ctypes.Structure):
      _fields_ = [('items', ctypes.POINTER (ctypes.c_char_p)),
               ('length', ctypes.c_int)]

   class CELL (ctypes.Structure):
      pass

   CELL._fields_ = [('index', ctypes.c_int), ('length',
ctypes.c_int),
               ('prev', ctypes.POINTER (CELL))]
```

A few notes:

- All structures are classes that inherit from ctypes.Structure.
- The only field _fields_is a list of tuples. Each tuple is (<varia-ble-name>, <ctypes.TYPE>).
- There ctypesare similar types in c_char (char) and c_char_p (* char) .
- There is ctypesalso one POINTER()that creates a type pointer from each type passed to it.
- If you have a recursive definition like in CELL, you must pass the initial declaration, and then add the fields _fields_in order to get a link to yourself later.
- Since I did not use CELLPython in my code, I did not need to write this structure, but it has an interesting property in the re-cursive field.

Call your code in C

In addition, I needed some code to convert Python types to new struc-tures in C. Now you can use your new C function to speed up Python code.

```python
def list_to_SEQUENCE (strlist: List [str]) -> SEQUENCE:
    bytelist = [bytes (s, 'utf-8') for s in strlist]
    arr = (ctypes.c_char_p * len (bytelist)) ()
    arr [:] = bytelist
    return SEQUENCE (arr, len (bytelist))


def lcs (s1: List [str], s2: List [str]) -> List[str]:
    seq1 = list_to_SEQUENCE(s1)
    seq2 = list_to_SEQUENCE(s2)

# struct Sequence * lcs (struct Sequence * s1, struct Sequence *
s2)
common = lcsmodule.lcs (ctypes.byref (seq1), ctypes.byref
(seq2)) [0]

    ret = []

    for i in range (common.length):
        ret.append (common.items [i] .decode ('utf-8')) lcsmo-
        dule.freeSequence (common)

    return ret

lcsmodule = ctypes.cdll.LoadLibrary ('lcsmodule / lcs.so')
lcsmodule.lcs.restype = ctypes.POINTER (SEQUENCE)

list1 = ['My', 'name', 'is', 'Sam', 'Stevens', '!']
list2 = ['My', 'name', 'is', 'Alex', 'Stevens', '.']

common = lcs (list1, list2)

print (common)

# ['My', 'name', 'is', 'Stevens']
```

A few notes:

- **char (list of strings) matches directly to a list of bytes in Python.
- There lcs.cis a function lcs()with the signature struct Sequence * lcs (struct Sequence * s1, struct Sequence
- s2) . To set up the return type, I use lcsmodule.lcs.restype = ctypes.POINTER(SEQUENCE).
- To make a call with a reference to the Sequence structure, I use ctypes.byref()one that returns a "light pointer" to your object (faster than ctypes.POINTER()).
- common.items- this is a list of bytes, they can be decoded to get retin the form of a list str.
- lcsmodule.freeSequence (common) just frees the memory associated with common. This is important because the garbage collector (AFAIK) will not automatically collect it.

Optimized Python code is code that you wrote in C and wrapped in Python.

Something More: PyPy

Attention: I myself have never used PyPy.

One of the simplest optimizations is to run your programs in the PyPyruntime, which contains a JIT compiler (just-in-time) that speeds up the work of loops, compiling them into machine code for repeated execution.

1. FINDING THE PERFECT TOOLKIT: ANALYZING POPULAR PYTHON PROJECT TEMPLATES

The materials, the translation of which we publish today, is dedicated to the story about the tools used to create Python applications. It is designed for those programmers who have already left the category of beginners but have not yet reached the category of experienced Python developers.

For those who can't wait to start practice, the author suggests using Flake8,pytest, and Sphinx in existing Python projects. He also recommends a look at pre-commit,Black, and Pylint. Those who plan to start a new project, he advises paying attention to Poetry and Dependable.

Overview

It has always been difficult for me to form an objective opinion about the "best practices" of Python development. In the world of technology, some popular trends are continually emerging, often not existing for long. This complicates the extraction of the "useful signal" from the information noise.

The freshest tools are often only good, so to speak, on paper. Can they help the practical programmer with something? Or their application only leads to the introduction of something new in the project, the performance of which must be maintained, which carries more difficulties than benefits?

I didn't have a clear understanding of what exactly I considered the "best practices" of development. I suppose I found something useful, based mainly on episodic evidence of "utility," and on the occasional mention of this in conversations. I decided to put things in order in this matter. To do this, I began to analyze all the templates of Python projects that I could find (we are talking about templates used by the cookiecuttercommand-line utility to create Python projects based on them).

It seemed to me that it was fascinating to learn about what auxiliary tools the template authors consider worthy of getting these tools into new Python projects created based on these templates.

I analyzed and compared the 18 most popular template projects (from 76 to 6300 stars on GitHub), paying particular attention to what kind of auxiliary tools they use. The results of this examination can be found in this table.

Below I want to share the main conclusions that I have made while analyzing popular templates.

De facto standards

The tools discussed in this section are included in more than half of the templates. This means that they are perceived as standard in a large number of real Python projects.

Flake8

I have been using Flake8 for quite some time, but I did not know about the dominant position in the field of linting that this tool occupies. I thought that it exists in a kind of competition, but the vast majority of project templates use it.

Yes, this is not surprising. It is difficult to oppose something to the convenience of linting the entire code base of the project in a matter of seconds. Those who want to use cutting-edge development can recommend a look at us make-python-style guide. This is something like "Flake8 on steroids." This tool may well contribute to the transfer to the category of obsolete other similar tools (like Pylint).

Pytest and coverage.py

The vast majority of templates use pytest. This reduces the use of the standard unit test framework. Pytest looks even more attractive when combined with tox. That's precisely what was done in about half of the templates. Code coverage with tests is most often checked using coverage.py.

Sphinx

Most templates use Sphinx to generate documentation. To my surprise, MkDocsis rarely used for this purpose.

As a result, we can say that if you do not use Flake8, pytest, and Sphinx in your current project, then you should consider introducing them.

Promising tools

In this section, I collected those tools and techniques, the use of which in the templates suggested some trends. The point is that although all this does not appear in most project templates, it is found in many relatively recent templates. So - all this is worth paying attention to.

Pyproject.toml

File usage is pyproject.tomlsuggested in PEP 518. This is a modern mechanism for specifying project assembly requirements. It is used in most fairly young templates.

Poetry

Although the Python ecosystem isn't doing well in terms of an excellent tool for managing dependencies, I cautiously optimistic that Poetry could be the equivalent of npm from the JavaScript world in the Python world.

The youngest (but popular) project templates seem to agree with this idea of mine. Real, it is worth saying that if someone is working on some kind of library that he can plan to distribute through PyPI, then he will still have to use setup tools. (It should to be noted that after the publication of this material, I was informed that this is no longer a problem).

Also, be careful if your project (the same applies to dependencies) relies on Conda. In this case, Poetry will not suit you, since this tool, in its current form, binds the developer to pip and virtualenv.

Dependabot

Dependabotregularly checks project dependencies for obsolescence and tries to help the developer by automatically opening PR.

I have recently seen this tool more often than before. It seems like to me that it is an excellent tool: the addition of which to the project affects the project very positively. Dependabot helps reduce security risks by pushing developers to keep dependencies up to date.

As a result, I advised you not to lose sight of Poetry and Dependabot. Consider introducing these tools into your next project.

Personal recommendations

Analysis of project templates gave me a somewhat ambivalent perception of the tools that I will list in this section. In any case, I want to use this section to tell about them, based on my own experience. At one time, they were beneficial to me.

Pre-commit

Even if you are incredibly disciplined - do not waste your energy on performing simple routine actions such as additional code run through the linter before sending the code to the repository. Similar tasks can be passed to Pre-commit. And it's better to spend your energy on TDD and teamwork on code.

Pylint

Although Pylint is criticized for being slow, although this tool is criticized for the features of its settings, I can say that it allowed me to grow above myself in the field of programming.

He gives me specific instructions on those parts of the code that I can improve, tells me how to make the code better comply with the rules. For a free tool, this alone is already very much. Therefore, I am ready to put up with the inconvenience associated with Pylint.

Black

Black at the root of the debate over where to put spaces in the code. This protects our teams from an empty talk and meaningless differences in files caused by different editors' settings.

In my case, it brightens up what I don't like about Python (the need to use a lot of spaces). Moreover, it should be noted that the Black project in 2019 joined the Python Software Foundation, which indicates the seriousness and quality of this project.

As a result, I want to say that if you still do not use pre-commit, Black, and Pylint - think about whether these tools can benefit your team.

Subtotals

Twelve of the eighteen investigated templates were created using the cookiecutterframework. Some of those templates where this framework is not used have exciting qualities.

But given the fact that cookiecutter is the leading framework for creating project templates, those who decide to use a template that did not use a cookiecutter should have excellent reasons for this. Such a decision should be very well justified.

Those who are looking for a template for their project should choose a template that most closely matches his view of things. If you, when creating projects according to a precise template, continuously have to reconfigure them in the same way, think about how to fork such a template and refine it, inspired by examples of templates from my list.

And if you are attracted to adventure - create your template from scratch. Cookiecutter is an excellent feature of the Python ecosystem, and the simple process of creating Jinja templates allows you to quickly and easily do something your own.

Bonus: Template Recommendations

Django

Together with the most popular Django templates, consider using we make-django-template. It gives the impression of a deeply thought out product.

Data Processing and Analysis

In most projects aimed at processing and analyzing data, the Cookiecutter Data Science template is useful. However, data scientists should also look at Kedro.

This template extends Cookiecutter Data Science with a mechanism for creating standardized data processing pipelines. It supports loading and saving data and models. These features are very likely to be able to find a worthy application in your next project.

Here I would also like to express my gratitude to the creators of the shablonatemplate for preparing very high- quality documentation. It can be useful to you even if you end up choosing something else.

General PurposeTemplates

Which general-purpose template to choose in some way depends on what exactly you are going to develop based on this template - a library or a regular application. But I, selecting a similar template, along with the most popular projects of this kind, would look very closely at Jace's Python Template.

This is not a well-known pattern, but I like the fact that it has Poetry, isort, Black, pylint, and mypy.

PyScaffoldis one of the most popular non-cookiecutter based templates. It has many extensions (for example, for Django, and Data Science projects). It also downloads version numbers from GitHub using setuptools-scm. Further, this is one of the few templates supporting Conda.

Here are a couple of templates that use GitHub Actions technology:

1. The Python Best Practices Cookiecutter template, which, I want to note, has most of my favorite tools.
2. The Blueprint / Boilerplate For Python Projects template, which I find pretty interesting, as the ability it gives them to find common security problems with Bandit, looks promising. Also, this template has a remarkable feature, which consists in the fact that the settings of all tools are collected in a single file setup.cfg.

And finally - I recommend taking a look at we make-python-package template. I think it's worth doing it anyway. In particular, if you like the Django template of the same developer, or if you are going to use the advanced, we make-python-style guide instead of pure Flake8.

3. HOW ARE BROAD INTEGER TYPES IMPLEMENTED IN PYTHON?

When you write in a low-level language such as C, you are worried about choosing the right data type and qualifiers for your integers, at each step, you analyze whether it will be enough to use it simply intor whether you need to add longor even long double. However, when writing code in Python, you don't need to worry about these "minor" things, because Python can work with numbers of integerany size type
.

In C, if you try to calculate 220,000 using the built-in function powl, you will get the output inf.

```
#include <stdio.h>
#include <math.h>

int main (void) {
   printf ("% Lf \ n", powl (2, 20000)):
   return 0:
}

$ ./a.out
inf
```

But in Python, making this easier than ever is easy:

```
>>> 2 ** 20,000
398027684033796659235430720619120245370477278049242593871134 ...

... 6021 digits long ...

6309376
```

It must be under the hood that Python is doing something very beautiful, and today we will find out the exactly what it does to work with integers of arbitrary size!

Presentation and Definition

Integer in Python, this is a C structure defined as follows:

```
struct _longobject {
    PyObject_VAR_HEAD
    digit ob_digit [1];
};
PyObject_VAR_HEADIs a macro, it expands to PyVarObject, which has the following structure:
typedef struct {
    PyObject ob_base;
    Py_ssize_t ob_size; /* Number of items in variable part */
} PyVarObject;
```

Other types that have PyObject_VAR_HEAD:

- PyBytesObject
- PyTupleObject
- PyListObject

This means that an integer, like a tuple or a list, has a variable length, and this is the first step to understanding how Python can support work with giant numbers. Once expanded, the macro _longobjectcan be considered as:

```
struct _longobject {
    PyObject ob_base;
    Py_ssize_t ob_size; /* Number of items in variable part */
    digit ob_digit [1];
};
```

There PyObjectare some meta fields in the structure that are used for reference counting (garbage collection), but to talk about this, we need a separate article. The field on which we will focus this ob_digitand in a bit ob_size.

Decoding ob_digit

ob_digitIs a statically allocated array of unit length of type digit (typedef для uint32_t). Since this is an array, it ob_digitis a pointer primarily to a number, and therefore, if necessary, it can be increased using the malloc function to any length. This way, python can represent and process very large numbers.

Typically, in low-level languages such as C, the precision of integers is limited to 64 bits. However, Python supports integers of arbitrary precision. Starting with Python 3, all numbers are presented in the form bignum and are limited only by the available system memory.

Decoding ob_size

ob_sizestores the number of items in ob_digit. Python overrides and then uses the value ob_sizeto to determine the actual number of elements contained in the array to increase the efficiency of allocating memory to the array ob_digit.

Storage

The most naive way to store integer numbers is to store one decimal digit in one element of the array. Operation such as additional and subtractions can be performed according to the rules of mathematics from elementary school.

With this approach, the number 5238 will be saved like this:

This approach is inefficient because we will use up to 32-bit digits (uint32_t) for storing a decimal digit, which ranges from 0 to 9 and can be easily represented with only 4 bits. After all, when writing something as universal like python, the kernel developer needs to be even more inventive.

So, can we do better? Of course, otherwise, we would not have posted this article. Let's take a closer look at how Python stores an extra-long integer.

Python path

Instead of storing only one decimal digit in each element of the array ob_digit, Python converts the numbers from the number system with base 10 to the numbers in the system with base 230 and calls each element as a number whose value ranges from 0 to 230 - 1.

In the hexadecimal number system, the base 16 ~ 24 means that each "digit" of the hexadecimal number ranges from 0 to 15 in the decimal number system. In Python, it's similar to a "number" with a base of 230, which means that the number will range from 0 to 230 - 1 = 1073741823 in decimal.

In this way, Python effectively uses almost all of the allocated space of 32 bits per digit, saves resources, and still performs simple operations, such as adding and subtracting at the math level of elementary school.

Depending on the platform, Python uses either 32-bit unsigned integer arrays or 16-bit unsigned integer arrays with 15-bit digits. To perform the operations that will be discussed later, you need only a few bits.

Example: 1152921504606846976

As already mentioned, for Python, numbers are represented in a system with a base of 230, that is, if you convert 1152921504606846976 into a number system with a base of 230, you will get 100.

1152 9215 0460 6846 976 = 1 * ((230) 2 + 0) * ((230) 1 + 0) *((230) 0)

Since it is the ob_digitfirst to store the least significant digit, it is stored as 001 in three digits. The structure _longobjectfor this value will contain:

- ob_size like 3
- ob_digit like [0, 0, 1]

We created a demo REPL that will show how Python stores an integer inside itself, and also refers to structural members such as ob_size, ob_refcountetc.

Integer Long Operations

Now that we have a pure idea of how Python implements integers of arbitrary precision, it is time to understand how various mathematical operations are performed with them.

Addition

Integers are stored "in numbers," which means that addition is as simple as in elementary school, and the Python source code shows us that this is how addition is implemented. A function with a name x_addin a file longobject.cadds two numbers.

```
For (i = 0; i < size_b; ++i) {
    carry += a->ob_digit [i] + b->ob_digit [i];
    z-> ob_digit [i] = carry & PyLong_MASK;
    carry >> = PyLong_SHIFT;
}
For  (; i < size_z; ++i) {
    carry += a->ob_digit [i];
    z-> ob_digit [i] = carry & PyLong _MASK;
    carry >> = PyLong_SHIFT;
}
z-> ob_digit [i] = carry;
```

The code snippet above is taken from a function x_add. As you can see, it iterates over a number by numbers and performs the addition of numbers, calculates the result and adds hyphenation.

It becomes more interesting when the result of addition is a negative number. The sign ob_sizeis an integer sign, that is, if you have a negative number, then it ob_sizewill be a minus. The value ob_sizemodulo will determine the number of digits in ob_digit.

Subtraction

Just as addition takes place, subtraction also takes place. A function with a name x_subin the file longobject.csubtracts one number from another.

```
For (i = 0; i < size_b; ++i) {
    borrow = a -> ob_digit [i] - b-> ob_digit [i] - borrow;
    z-> ob_digit [i] = borrow & PyLong_MASK;
    borrow >> = PyLong_SHIFT;
    borrow & = 1; /* Keep only one sign bit */
}
for (; i <size_a; ++i) {
    borrow = a-> ob_digit [i] - borrow;
    z-> ob_digit [i] = borrow & PyLong_MASK;
    borrow >> = PyLong_SHIFT;
    borrow & = 1; /* Keep only one sign bit */
}
```

The code snippet above is taken from a function x_sub. In it, you see how the enumeration of numbers occurs and subtraction is performed, the result is calculated and the transfer is distributed. Indeed, it is very similar to addition.

Multiplication

And again, the multiplication will be implemented in the same naive way that we learned from the lessons of mathematics in elementary school, but it is not very efficient. To maintain efficiency, Python implements theKaratsuba algorithm, which multiplies two n-digit numbers in O (nlog23) simple steps.

The algorithm is not simple and its implementation is beyond the scope of this article, but you can find its implementation in functions and in the file .k_mulk_lopsided_mullongobject.c

Division and other operations

All operations on integers are defined in the file longobject.c, they are very simple to find and trace the work of each. Attention: A detailed understanding of the work of each of them will take time, so pre-stock up with popcorn.

Optimizing Frequently Used Integers

Python preallocatesa small number of integers in memory ranging from -5 to 256. This allocation occurs during initialization, and since we cannot change integers (immutability), these pre-allocated numbers are singleton and are directly referenced instead of being allocated. This means that every time we use/create a small number, Python instead of reallocation simply returns a reference to the previously allocated number.

Such optimization can be traced in the macro IS_SMALL_INTand function get_small_intclongobject.c. So Python saves a lot of space and time in calculating commonly used integer numbers.

4. CREATE A BOT IN PYTHON TO LEARN ENGLISH

No, this is not one of the hundreds of articles on how to write your first Hello World bot in Python. Here you will not find detailed instructions on how to get an API token in BotFather or launch a bot in the cloud. In return, we will show you how to unleash the full power of Python to the maximum to achieve the most aesthetic and beautiful code. We perform a song about the appeal of complex structures - we dance and dance. Under the cut asynchrony, its system of saves, a bunch of useful decorators, and a lot of beautiful code.

Disclaimer: People with brain OOP and adherents of the "right" patterns may ignore this article.

Idea

To understand what it is like not to know English in modern society, imagine that you are an 18th-century nobleman who does not know French. Even if you are not very well versed in history, you can still imagine how hard it would be to live under such circumstances. In the modern world, English has become a necessity, not a privilege, especially if you are in the IT industry.

The project is based on the catechism of the future: the development of a neural network as a separate unit, and education, which is based on games and sports spirit. Isomorphic paradigms have been hanging in the air since ancient times, but it seems that over time, people began to forget that the most straightforward solutions are the most effective.

Here is a shortlist of the basic things I want to put together:

- Be able to work with three user dictionaries
- Ability to parse youtube video/text, and then add new words to the user's dictionary
- Two basic skills training modes

- Flexible customization: full control over user dictionaries and the environment in general
- Built-in admin panel

Naturally, everything should work quickly, with the ability to easily replenish existing functionality in the future. Putting it all together, I thought that the best embodiment of my idea into reality would be a Telegram bot. My tale is not about how to write handlers for the bot correctly - there are dozens of such articles, and this is simple mechanical work. I want the reader to learn to ignore the typical dogmas of programming. Use what is profitable and effective here and now.

"I learned to let out the cries of unbelievers past my ears because it was impossible to suppress them."

Base structure

The bot will be based on the python-telegram-bot (ptb) library. I use loguru as a logger , though there is one small snag here. The fact is that ptb by default uses a different logger (standard logging) and does not allow you to connect your own. Of course, it would be possible to intercept all journal messages globally and send them to our registrar, but we will do it a little easier:

```
from loguru import logger
import sys

# Configure dual-stream output to the console and to the file
config = {
    'handlers': [
        {'sink': sys.stdout, 'level': 'INFO'},
        {'sink': 'logs.log', 'serialize': False, 'level': 'DEBUG'},
    ]
}

logger.configure(**config)

# ...

updater = Updater('YOUR_TOKEN')
dp = updater.dispatcher

# Roughly fasten your logger. Cheap and cheerful
updater.logger = logger
dp.logger = logger
```

Unfortunately, I don't have the opportunity to deploy my bot on stable data centers, so data security is a priority. For these purposes, I implemented my system of saves. It provides flexible and convenient work with data - statistics collection, as an example of easy replenishment of functionality in the future.

```python
from __future__ import annotations # In the future, I will omit this import
from loguru import logger

import inspect
import functools
import os

def file_is_empty (path: str) -> bool:
    return os.stat (path).st_size == 0

def clear_file (path: str) -> None:
    with open (path, 'w'): pass

def cache_decorator (method):
    @ functools.wraps (method)
    def wrapper (self, * args, ** kwargs):
        res = method (self, * args, ** kwargs)
        Cache.link.recess (self, {'method_name': method __name__}) # (1)
        # During testing, multiple calls can slow down
        # program work: opt avoids this
        logger.opt (lazy = True) .debug (f'Decorator for {method __name__} was end ')
        return res
    return wrapper

class cache:
    ..
```

+ cache_size - Std thfDtlgh 'hi ch dl data will be su'ed

+ cache_files - Dump file in w'hich all intermediate operations on data are stored

link = None

```
def      init      (self. cache_size =10):
             = Save all screw'edcl asses. This all or'syout oflexibl›' vorkwith data.
             self. cl asses = []
             =Files matching classes
             sel f._cache_fi1es = []
        = (1). A smdl hack that dl or'syou to cd1 a specifi c instance
        thrDtlgha common class
        = This w'wksbecause w'eoril\' have one instance Df the cl ass. 'hi ch
        = implements d 1 the logic of 'orkingwith data. In addition. it is conve-
        nient arid all o 's
        = stgum cantl›' expand the functlDflallt›' in the future
        sel f. cl ass .link= self


        self._counter = 0
            self.CACHESIZE = cache stze
```

```
def add (self, d s: class, file: str) ->NDne:

    All or's to fasten a class to a saver

    + cls- Inst anceof the class
    + file - The fi1 e the instariceis 'orkingwith

    self._cache_files.append (file)
    self._classes.append(cls)

    if fi1e is eotptl' (fi1e): return hDne

    1ogger.opt dan.'=True).debug(fTor{cls.          classnames)      file
    (file) is not empty' ')

    fa data in sells oad(file):
    is.savenDnCaclting (data)


    cl ear_file (file)
    self._counter = 0


def recess (self, cls: ctass, data diet) —>Ncrie:

    The main method that performs the basic l o c of saves

    if self. counter + 1/ = self.CACHESIZE:
    self.saveall 0
    el se:
            self._counter+ = I
            fil ename= self._cache_files [self._classes.index (cls)]
            self.save(data. fil enam e = filename)


= For simplicit›', save_d1, save, load methods are omitted
```

Now we can create any methods that can modify data, without fear of losing important data:

```
@cache_decorator
def add_smth_important (* args, ** kwargs) -> Any:
    # ...
    # We make some important actions on the data ...
    # ...
```

Now that we have figured out the basic structure, the main question remains: how to put everything together. I implemented the main class - EnglishBot, which brings together the entire primary structure: PTB, work with the database, the save system, and which will manage the whole business logic of the bot. If the implementation of Telegram commands were simple, we could easily add them to the same class. But, unfortunately, their organization occupies most of the code of the entire application, so adding them to the same class would be crazy. I also did not want to create new classes/subclasses, because I suggest using a very simple structure:

```
# Import the main class
from modules import EnglishBot
# Import classes that implement Telegram commands
from modules.module import start
# ...

if __name__ == '__main__':
    # Initialize the bot
    tbot = EnglishBot (
        # ...
    )

    # Add handlers to the stack
    tbot.add_command_handler (start, 'start')
    # ...
```

How command modules get access to the main class, we will consider further.

All out of nothing

Ptb handlers have two arguments - update and context, which store all the necessary information stack. Context has a wonderful chat_data argument that can be used as a data storage dictionary for chat. But I do not want to constantly refer to it in a format context.chat_data['data']. I would like something light and beautiful, say context.data. However, this is not a problem.

```
from telegram.ext import CommandHandler

def a (self, key: str):
    # First, check if the class has the required value
    # If not, then try to return it from chat_data
    try:
        return object __ getattribute __ (self, key)
    except:
        return self.chat_data [key]

def b (self, key: str, data = None, replace = True):
    #Small hack: if replace = False and data exists, then overwriting does not occur
    # In this case, if the data is not specified, then they are put in None
    if replace or not self.chat_data.get (key, None):
        self.chat_data [key] = data

# Bindim context to receive data in the format context.data
CallbackContext __ getattribute __ = a
# As well as a convenient setter for your needs
CallbackContext.set = b
```

We continue to simplify our lives. Now I want all the necessary information for a specific user to be in quick access context.

```
def bind_context (func):
    def wrapper (update, context):
        context._bot.bind_user_data (update, context) # (2)
        return func (update, context)
    return wrapper

class EnglishBot:
    # ...

    def bind_user_data (self, update, context) -> dict:
        context.set ('t_id', update.message.chat_id, replace = False)
        context.set ('t_ln', update.message.from_user.language_code, replace = False)
        # ...
        # Set all the necessary information that we want to have quick access from context
        # For example, something from the database
        # ...
```

Now we'll completely become impudent and fasten our bot instance to context:

```
class EnglishBot:
    # ...

    def __init__ (self, * args, ** kwargs):
        # ...
        # (2): Now we can access the instance in the format context._bot
        CallbackContext._bot = self
```

We put everything in place and get a citadel of comfort and convenience in just one call.

```
from EnglishBot import bind_context

@bind_context
def start (update, context):
    # Now we have access to everything from one place
    # For example, we can easily add a new user to the database
    # Check if the user is in our database
    if not context._bot.user_exist (context.t_id):
        # For example, add some important notifications
        context.set ('push_notification', True)
        # And then add the user to the database
        context._bot.new_user (context.t_id, context.t_ln)

    return update.message.reply_text ('Welcome')
    # ...
```

Decorators are our everything

Most often, it turns out that the name of the function coincides with the name of the command to which we want to add a handler. Why not use this statistical feature for your selfish purposes.

```
class EnglishBot:
    # ...

    def add_command_handler (self, func: function, name = None) -> None:
        """
        Function that adds a command handler
        """

        name = name or func.__name__
        self.dp.add_handler (CommandHandler (name, func))

    # ...

# In the main file:
tbot.add_command_handler (start) # Instead of tbot.add_command_handler (start, 'start')
```

It looks cool, but it doesn't work. It's all about the bind_context decorator, which will always return the name of the wrapper function. Correct this misunderstanding.

```
import functools

def bind_context (func):
    # functools.wraps from stdlib saves signatures since Python 3.4
    @functools.wraps (func)
    def wrapper (update, context):
        context._bot.bind_user_data (update, context)
        return func (update, context)
    return wrapper
```

There are many message handlers in the bot, which, by design, should cancel the command when entering zero. Also I need to discard all edited posts.

```python
import functools

END = -1

def zero_exiter (func):
    @ functools.wraps (func)
    def wrapper (update, context):
        if update.to_dict () ['message']. get ('text', None) == '0':
            update.message.reply_text ('Sending some message')
            return END

        return func (update, context)
    return wrapper

def skip_edited (func):
    @ functools.wraps (func)
    def wrapper (update, context):
        # This works in all cases, because None returned
        # in the conversation_handler stack, leaves the function in its current state
        if not update.to_dict (). get ('edited_message', None):
            return func (update, context)
    return wrapper
```

We do not forget at the same time about the most important decorator - @run_asyncon which asynchrony is based. Now we collect the heavy function.

```python
from telegram.ext.dispatcher import run_async
from EnglishBot import skip_edited

@run_async
@skip_edited
def heavy_function (update, context):
    # ...
    # A heavy computing function that needs asynchrony
    # Has post edit protection
    # ...
```

Remember that asynchrony is a Jedi sword, but with this sword, you can quickly kill yourself.

Sometimes programs freeze without sending anything to the log. @logger.catch, the last decorator on our list, ensures that any error is correctly reported to a logger.

```python
from loguru import logger

@ logger.catch
def heavy_function2 (update, context):
    # ...
    # Another heavy computing function on which a program may hang
    # ...
```

Admin panel

Let's implement an admin panel with the ability to receive/delete logs and send a message to all users.

```python
from EnglishBot import bind_context
from Cache import file_is_empty
from telegram import ReplyKeyboardMarkup
from loguru import logger

LOG_FILE = 'logs.log'
SENDING, MAIN, END = range (1, -2, -1)

buttons = ReplyKeyboardMarkup (
    [('Get logs', 'logs'), ('Clear logs', 'clear')],
    [('Send message', 'send')],
    # [...],
)

@bind_context
def admin_panel (update, context):
    # Check user admin rights
    if not context._bot.acess_check (context.t_id):
        # A good security practice is to show the user that such a command does not exist
        return update.message.reply_text (f'Unknown command {update.message.text} ')

    update.message.reply_text ('Choose an option', reply_markup = buttons)

    return MAIN
```

```
!fi ero exiter
def send d1 (updast    context).
    count = 0
```

```
!fi ero exiter
def send d1 (updast    context).
    count = 0
```

```
def get logs (update context).
    if fil e is empU.' (LOG FILE).
        update.cd1back quo.'.rep1>' text
             are empU.") else.
      = Show' document loading
        context.bot.send chat  acti ‹xi
        (chat  id =  context.t  icL  action
        = 'upload  docum cut')
        context.bot.sendDocument (chat i
        d = context.t  icL docimi cut =
        open (L OG FILE 'rb') name = L
        Ohr  FILE
time‹xit = 1000)
```

```
  = Since we do not cl ose the admin
    panel you need to rem ove the
    dourload icon on the button
    update.cd1back quell'.answer (text
    = ")
  = B asicd1\' thi s is urin ecessm.'. As I
  sai d earli er None does not change the
  positi on of the hand er
  = But this was' the code locks much
    m‹xe readabl e return ñIAIN
```

```
def logs d ear (update context).
    with open (LOG FILE 'u") as fil e.
        update.cd1back quo.'.rep1>' text
        ('O ear ed) update.cd1back
        quo.'.answer (text = ")
```

```
    return ñIAIN
```

= Send methods

```
def take message (update context).
    update.cd1back quell'.rep1>' text
    ('Send m essag e) update.cd1back
    quell'.answer (text = ")
```

```
    return SENDING
```

```
!fi ero exiter
def send d1 (updast   context).
  count = 0
```

Get user identifi cfs from the
database for id in li st (context.
bot.get user ids Q).
= It may' happen that some user
has added a bet to the em ergenc\'
= Then when to.'ing to send him a
message an error u411 be caught
to.'.
= fi'e do not setid a message to
oursel ves if i d   context.t icL
continue
= Be sure to use ñlarkdour to
save message formatting
context.bet.send message
(context.t icL text =
update.message.text markdour
parse mode = ñlarkdour')
count + = 1
except. pass

update.cd1back quell'.rep1›' text
(£Sent to { count) pecpl e ')
update.cd1back quell'.answer (text
= ")

```
#
# In the main file.
tbot.add_conversation_handler (
    entry_points = [('admin', admin)].
    # The regularity for send_alk allows you to process any message that does not start with /
    states = [[(logs, " logs $"), (logs_clear, " clear $"), (send, " send $')], [(send_alk, '@ ^ ((?! * (( ^ ` /) +)). *)( ~) $
')]]
)
```

The add_conversation_handler function allows you to add a conversation handler in a minimalistic way:

```
class EnglishBot
    #...

    def add_conversation_handler (self, entry_points: list, states: list, fallbacks: list) -> None:
        fallbacks = [CommandHandler (name, func) for name, func in fallbacks]
        entry_points = [CommandHandler (name, func) for name, func in entry_points]
        r_states = {}

        for i in range (len (states)):
            r_states [i] = []

            # Each array describes functions of one state
            for func, pattern in states [i]:
                # If the regular starts with the @ symbol, then we add a message handler
                # Otherwise, a regular button handler
                if pattern [0] == '@':
                    r_states [i] .append (MessageHandler (Filters.regex (pattern [1:]), func))
                else:
                    r_states [i] .append (CallbackQueryHandler (func, pattern = pattern))

        conv_handler = ConversationHandler (entry_points = entry_points, states = r_states, fallbacks = fallbacks)
        dp.add_handler (conv_handler)
```

Main functionality

Let's teach our bot to add new words to user dictionaries.

```
from EnglishBot import bind_context, skip_edited, zero_exiter
from youtube_transcript_api import YouTubeTranscriptApi
from telegram.ext.dispatcher import run_async

START_OVER, ADDING, END = range (1, -2, -1)

re_youtube = re.compile ('^ (http (s)?: \/ \/)? ((w) {3} .)? youtu (be | .be)? (\. com)? \/.+' )
re_text = re.compile ('^ [æz] {3,20} $')

def is_youtube_link (link: str) -> bool:
    if re_youtube.match (link) is not None: return True
for s in bad_symbols:
def clear_text (text: str) -> str:
    bad_symbols = '! @ #% $ ^ & * () _ + 1234567890 - = /| \?> <, ":' ~ [] {}'
```

```python
        text = text.replace (s. ")

    return text.stra  ()  IDS'& ()


!@skip_edited
:@bind_context
def add_w'ords (update. context).
    update.message.reply' text ('Enter text:')
    return ADDING


:H uri_asx'nc
:@skip_edit ed
:@zero_exiter
def parse_text (update. context):
    DDDM DZténg takes soote titzte, sD ñ'ou need tD T1ctT1' the user that e\' .'thing is fine
    message = update.message.repl>'_text ('L oad rig ...')

    if is 'outube_link (update.message.text):
        = If the video is irivdid or there are no subtitl es in it, then we will catch ari  error
        to.':
            transcript list = Y en TubeTranscriptApi list transcripts (get sli deD id (update.message.text))
            t = tr ariscript_listfnd_transcript (['en'])
            _tmt = clear_tmt  ('.' .j » ([i [tmt'] fur i in tletJ  0])}  split ()
        ex cept:
            otessag z edtt text ('k\'âtid x'ideD. To.' again:')
            return ADD UG
    else:
        _text = clear_tnt (update.message.text) .split ()

    =  ¥Ve get  a link to the words the user alread>' has
        T'& ds.'  CDotext.  bDt.get ck ct 'ords (cDIttWt.t id)
        l 'ards tD be ad6ed
    good_w'ords = []
    = Discarded  words
    bad_words = Q

    = First, w'e discard duplicates
    for word in set   text):
        = Then  w'e check the correctness of the w'ord regular
        z = re_text.match (word)
        if z.
            = Add a vord onl>'if it is n ot already' in the user ñ ation m.'
            if z.group () net in _w'ords:
                good_wcrds.append (word)
            el se:
                bad_words.append  ('ord)

    = The Dnl >' thi Hg left 1 S tD suggest the user tD Add ends
    = And then add them t o the di cti Dfl .'
```

.. In the main file:
```
    tbot.add_coriversation_handler (
        entr>'  oints = [('add_wcrds', add_  'crds)],
```

```
states = [
    [(parse_text. '@ ^ ((7). * (('\() +)). *) (. +) $')].
    #
])
```

We pack the bot

Before we pack our bot, add proxy support and change log levels from the console.

```
# In the main file:

import argparse

parser = argparse.ArgumentParser ()
parser.add_argument ('-l', '--level', default = 'INFO',
          choices = ['TRACE', 'DEBUG', 'INFO', 'SUCCESS', 'WARNING', 'ERROR', 'CRITICAL'],
          help = 'Allows you to enable the bot in a given mode')
parser.add_argument ('- p', '--proxy', help = 'Allows you to enable bot with proxy')
args = parser.parse_args ()

config = {
  'handlers': [
    {'sink': sys.stdout, 'level': args.level},
    # It's not a mistake. In the file I collect logs of level DEBUG and higher
    {'sink': logs.log', 'serialize': False, 'level': DEBUG'},
  ]
}

logger.configure (** config)

if args.proxy:
    t_proxy = {'proxy_url': args.proxy, 'read_timeout': 1000, 'connect_timeout': 1000}
    # ...
    # Proxies for other services
    # ...
else:
    t_proxy = None
```

Python 3.5+ supports the ability to pack a directory into a single executable file. Let's take this opportunity to be able to deploy your work environment on any VPS easily. First, get the dependency file. If you are using a virtual environment, it can be done with one command: pip freeze > requirements.txt. If the project does not have a virtual environment, then you will have to tinker a bit. You can try to use pip freeze and manually isolate all the necessary packages. Still, if too many packages are installed on the system, then this method will not work. The second option is to use ready-made solutions, for example, pipreqs.

Now that our dependency file is ready, we can pack our directory into a .pyzfile. To do this, enter the command py - m zipapp "ПУТЬ_К_КАТАЛОГУ"   -m "ИМЯ_ГЛАВНОГО_ФАЙЛА:ГЛАВНАЯ_ФУНКЦИЯ" -o bot.pyz, it will create the bot.pyz file in the project folder. Please note that the code in init .py must be wrapped in some function, otherwise the executable file will be impossible to compile.

```
# Sample _init_ py file
# py -m zipapp "PATH_TO_CATALOG" -m "_init_.py:main" -o bot.pyz

def main ():
    #_

if _name_ == '_main_':
    main ()
```

We wrap the files in the archive zip bot.zip requirements.txt bot.pyzand send it to our VPS.

5. THE THERMAL IMAGER ON THE RASPBERRY PI

Well-known thermal imaging modules appeared on the famous Chinese site. Is it possible to assemble an exotic and, possibly, even useful thing - a home-made thermal imager? Why not, like Raspberry was lying somewhere. What came of it – I will tell you under the cut.

MLX90640. What is it?

And this, in fact, is a thermal imaging matrix with a microcontroller on board. Production of the previously unknown company Melexis. The thermal imaging matrix has a dimension of 32 by 24 pixels. This is not much, but when interpolating the image, it seems to be enough to make out something, at least.

There are two type of sensor is available version, the cases of which differ in the viewing angle of the matrix. A more squat structure A overlooks the outside world at an angle of 110 (horizontal) at 75 (vertical) degrees. B - under 55 by 37.5 degrees, respectively. The device case has only four outputs - two for power, two for communicating with the control device via the I2C interface. Interested datasheets can be downloaded here.

And then what is the GY-MCU90640?

Chinese comrades put the MLX90640 on board with another micro-controller on board (STM32F103). Apparently, for easier matrix management. This whole farm is called GY-MCU90640. And it costs at the time of acquisition (end of December 2018) in the region of 5 thousands $. As follows:

As you see, there are two types of boards, with a narrow or wide-angle version of the sensor onboard.

Which version is best for you? A good question, unfortunately, I had it only after the modules was already ordered and received. For some reason, at this time of the orders, I did not pay attention to these nuances. But in vain.

A wider version will be useful on self-propelled robots or in security system (the field of view will be larger). According to the datasheets, it also has less noise and higher measurement accuracy.

But for visualization tasks, I would more recommend a more "long-range" version of B. For one very significant reason. In the future, when shooting, it can be deployed (manually or on a platform with a drive) and take composite "photos," thereby increasing the more than a modest resolution of 32 by 24 pixels. Collects thermal images 64 by 96 pixels, for example. Well, all right, in the future, the photos will be from the wide-angle version A.

Connect to Raspberry PI

There are two ways to control the thermal imaging module:

1. Shorten the "SET" jumper on the board and use I2C to contact the internal microcontroller MLX90640 directly.
2. Leave the jumper alone and communicate with the module through a similar interface installed on the STM32F103 board via RS-232.

If you write in C ++, it will probably be more convenient to ignore the extra microcontroller, short-circuit the jumper and use the API from the manufacturer, which lies here.

Humble pythonists can also go the first way. It seems like that there are a couple of Python libraries (here and here). But unfortunately, not a single one worked for me.

Advanced pythonists can write a module control driver in Python. The procedure for obtaining a frame is described in detail in the datasheet. But then you will have to prescribe all the calibration procedures, which seems slightly burdensome. Therefore, I had to go the second way. It turned out to be moderately thorny, but quite passable.

Thanks to the insight of Chinese engineers or just a happy coincidence, the shawl turned out to have a perfect location of the conclusions:

It remains only to put the block and insert the scarf into the raspberry connector. A 5 to 3 Volt converter is installed on the board, so it seems that nothing threatens Raspberry's delicate Rx and Tx terminals.

It should be added that the connection according to the first option, is also possible, but requires more labor and solder skill. The board must be installed on the other side of the Raspberry connector (shown in the title photo of this post).

Soft

On a well-known Chinese site, such a miracle is offered to access the GY-MCU90640:

Most likely, there should be some description of the interaction protocol with the microcontroller installed on the board, according to which this software product works! After a brief conversation with the seller of scarves (respect to these respected gentlemen), such a protocol was sent to me. It appeared in pdf and pure Chinese.

Thanks to Google's translator and active copy-paste, after about an hour and a half, the protocol was decrypted, anyone can read it on Github. It turned out that the scarf understands six basic commands, among which there is a frame request on the COM port.

Each pixel of the matrix is, in fact, the temperature value of the object that this pixel is looking at. The temperature in degrees Celsius times 100 (double-byte number). There is even a special mode in which the scarf will send frames from the matrix to the Raspberry 4 times per second.

```
import numpy as np
import cv2

    d function to get Emissivity from MCU
    def get_emissivity ():
      ser.write(semi d .to_bytes([0xA5,Dx55 ,0xOl ,OxFB]))

read = ser.read(4) return read [2] / 100

d function to gatemperatures from MCU (Celsius degree x 100)
<Ref ga_temp_oray(d):

# getting ambient tame
T_a= (iot(d[1540]) + int (d [1541]) • 256) / 100

# getting raw array of pixels temperie
raw_data= d [4: 1540]
T_array=npJrombtdfa(raw_            . dtype= up.intl6)
```

```
rcturaT_a,T_anay

#fiioaiontoconverttemplestopixelsoaimage
def td_to_image(f).
norm = up.nint8 ((f. 100 - Twin) • 255, (Tmax-Tmin))
norm.shy= (24.32)
```

============================== Main cycle ========================

Color map range
```
Tn   =40
Tmin=20


    print ('Corifi guring Seri d port')
    ser = seri d .Seri d (' dev ." seri d 0')
    ser.baucYate = 115200

  = set frequency' of module to 4 Hz
    ser.site (seri d.to baies ([0xA5 0x25 0x01 0xCB]))
    time.sleep (0.1)

  = Starting automati c data colecti on
    ser.site (seri d.to baies ([0xA5 0x35 0x02 0xD/)
    t0 = time.time Q


    while True.
  = waiting for data frame
    data = ser.read (1544)

  = The data is ready' l et's handle it!
    To tanp array' = get temp  array' (data)
    ta img = td to image (temp array')

  = Guage processing
    img = cv2.applvColorñlap (ta imgcv2.COL ORñfAP JE T)
    img = cv2.rest ze (inn g (320 240) interpolati on = cv2.IhMR  GB  IC)
    img = cv2 Hi p (inn g l)
    text = Tmin = {. +. 1f) Tmax  = {. +. 1f) FPS = {. .2f)'. format (temp
    array'.min ()." 100 temp array'.max Q ." 100
    1 ." (time .time Q - t0))
    cv2.putText (img text (5 15) cv2.FONT HERSHEY SET&LE X 0.45 (0
    0 0) 1)
    cv2.imshou' ('Output' img)

  * if 's' is pressed - savi ng of picture key' = cv2.waitKe\' (1) & 0xFF
    if key'    ord (" s").
    fname = 'pic ' + dt.datetime.now' Q. strfli me (". o Y-°. o m-°. » d °. » H-°. » ñI-
    °. » S) + '.jpg' cv2.imuñte (fnam e img)
    print ('Savi rig image' fnam e) t0 = time.time Q
```

```
except KevboardInterrupt.
* to terminate the cycle
ser.site (seri d.to baies ([0xA5 0x35 0x01 0xDB])) ser.close Q
cv2.destrovAllfi'indows Q print ('Stopped)

= just in case ser.close Q
cv2.destrovAllfi'indows Q
```

Results

The script polls the thermal imaging matrix and outputs the frames to the monitor console on which the Raspberry PI is connected, four times per second. This is enough not to experience significant discomfort when shooting objects. To visualize the frame, the OpenCV package is used. When the "s" button is pressed, the thermal imaging "heat maps" in jpg format are saved in the folder with the script.

For more information, I deduced the minimum and maximum temperatures on the frame. That is, looking at the color, you can see what approximately the temperature of the most heated or chilled objects. The measurement error is approximately a degree with a larger side. The thermal range is set from 20 to 40 degrees. Exit the script by pressing Ctrl + C.

The script works approximately the same on both the Raspberry Pi Zero W and the Pi 3 B +. I installed the VNC server on the smartphone. Thus, picking up raspberries connected to a power bank and a smartphone with VNC running, you can get a portable thermal imager with the ability to save thermal images. Perhaps this is not entirely convenient, but quite functional.

After the first start, an incorrect measurement of the maximum temperature is possible. In this case, you need to exit the script and rerun it.

That is all for today. The experiment with a home-made thermal imager turned out to be successful. With the helping of this device, it is quite possible to conduct a thermal imaging inspection of the house on your own, for example.

Due to the lower temperature contrast than indoors, the pictures were not very informative. In the photo above, the whole house is on two sides. On the bottom - photos of different windows.

In the code, I changed only the temperature range. Instead of +20 ... + 40, I set -10 ... + 5.

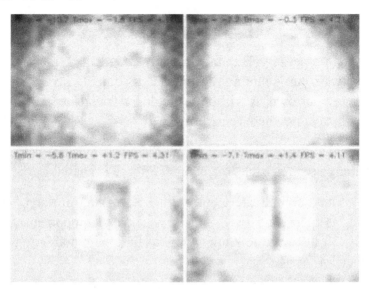

6. FINDING A FREE PARKING SPACE WITH PYTHON

I live in a proper city. But, like in many others, the search for a parking space always turns into a test. Free spaces quickly occupy, and even if you have your own, it will be difficult for friends to call you because they will have nowhere to park.

So I decided to point the camera out the window and use deep learning so that my computer tells me when the space is available:

It may sound complicated, but writing a working prototype with deep learning is quick and easy. All the necessary components are already there - you just need to know where to find them and how to put them together.

So let's have some fun and write an accurate free parking notification system using Python and deep learning

Decomposing the task

When we have a difficult task that we want to solve with the help of machine learning, the first step is to break it down into a sequence of simple tasks. Then we can use various tools to solve each of them. By combining several simple solutions, we get a system that is capable of something complex.

Here is how I broke my task:

The video stream from the webcam directed to the window enters the conveyor input: Through the pipeline, we will transmit each frame of the video, one at a time.

The first point is to recognize all the possible parking spaces in the frame. Before we can look for unoccupied places, we need to understand in which parts of the image there is parking.

Then on each frame you need to find all the cars. This will allow us to track the movement of each machine from frame to frame.

The third step is to determine which places are occupied by machines and which are not. To do this, combine the results of the first two steps.

Finally, the program should send an alert when the parking space becomes free. This will be determined by changes in the location of the machines between the frames of the video.

Each of the step can be completed in different ways using different technologies. There is no single right or wrong way to compose this conveyor: different approaches will have their advantages and disadvantages. Let's deal with each step in more detail.

We recognize parking spaces

Here is what our camera sees:

We need to scan this image somehow and get a list of places to park:

The solution "in the forehead" would be to simply hardcode the locations of all parking spaces manually instead of automatically recognizing them. But in this case, if we move the camera or want to look for parking spaces on another street, we will have to do the whole procedure again. It sounds so-so, so let's look for an automatic way to recognize parking spaces.

Alternatively, you can search for parking meters in the image and assume that there is a parking space next to each of them:

However, with this approach, not everything is so smooth. Firstly, not every parking space has a parking meter, and indeed, we are more interested in finding parking spaces for which you do not have to pay. Secondly, the location of the parking meter does not tell us anything about where the parking space is, but it only allows us to make an assumption.

Another idea is to create an object recognition model that looks for parking space marks drawn on the road:

But this approach is so-so. Firstly, in my city, all such trademarks are very small and difficult to see at a distance, so it will be difficult to detect them using a computer. Secondly, the street is full of all sorts of other lines and marks. It will be challenging to separate parking marks from lane dividers and pedestrian crossings.

When you encounter a problem that at first glance seems complicated, take a few minutes to find another approach to solving the problem, which will help to circumvent some technical issues. What is the parking space? This is just a place where a car is parked for a long time. Perhaps we do not need to recognize parking spaces at all. Why don't we acknowledge only cars that have stood still for a long time and not assume that they are standing in a parking space?

In other words, parking spaces are located where cars stand for a long time:

Thus, if we can recognize the cars and find out which of them do not move between frames, we can guess where the parking spaces are. Simple as that - let's move on to recognizing cars!

Recognize cars

Recognizing cars on a video frame is a classic object recognition task. There are many machine learning approaches that we could use for recognition. Here are some of them in order from the "old school" to the "new school":

- You can train the detector based on HOG (Histogram of Oriented Gradients, histograms of directional gradients) and walk it through the entire image to find all the cars. This old approach, which does not use deep learning, works relatively quickly but does not cope very well with machines located in different ways.

- You can train a CNN-based detector (Convolutional Neural Network, a convolutional neural network) and walk through the entire image until you find all the cars. This approach works precisely, but not as efficiently since we need to scan the image several times using CNN to find all the machines. And although we can find machines located in different ways, we need much more training data than for a HOG detector.

- You can use a new approach with deep learning like Mask R-CNN, Faster R-CNN, or YOLO, which combines the accuracy of CNN and a set of technical tricks that significantly increase the speed of recognition. Such models will work relatively quickly (on the GPU) if we have a lot of data for training the model.

In the general case, we need the simplest solution, which will work as it should and require the least amount of training data. This is not required to be the newest and fastest algorithm. However, specifically in our case, Mask R- CNN is a reasonable choice, even though it is unique and fast.

Mask R-C-N-N architecture is designed in such a way that it recognizes objects in the entire image, effectively spending resources, and does not use the sliding window approach. In other words, it works pretty fast. With a modern GPU, we can recognize objects in the video in high resolution at a speed of several frames per second. For our project, this should be enough.

Also, Mask R-CNN provides a lot of information about each recognized object. Most recognition algorithms return only a bounding box for each object. However, Mask R-CNN will not only give us the location of each object but also its outline (mask):

To train Mask R-CNN, we need a lot of images of the objects that we want to recognize. We could go outside, take pictures of cars, and mark them in photographs, which would require several days of work. Fortunately, cars are one of those objects that people often want to recognize, so several public datasets with images of cars already exist.

One of them is the popular SOCO dataset (short for Common Objects In Context), which has images annotated with object masks. This dataset contains over 12,000 images with already labeled machines. Here is an example image from the dataset:

Such data is excellent for training a model based on Mask R-CNN.

But hold the horses, there is news even better! We are not the first who wanted to train their model using the COCO dataset - many people had already done this before us and shared their results. Therefore, instead of training our model, we can take a ready-made one that can already recognize cars. For our project, we will use the open-sourcemodel from Matterport.

If we give the image from the camera to the input of this model, this is what we get already "out of the box":

The model recognized not only cars but also objects such as traffic lights and people. It's funny that she recognized the tree as a house-plant.

For each recognized object, the Mask R-CNN model returns four things:

- Type of object detected (integer). The pre-trained COCO model can recognize 80 different everyday objects like cars and trucks. A complete list is available here.
- The degree of confidence in the recognition results. The higher the number, the stronger the model is confident in the correct recognition of the object.
- Abounding box for an object in the form of XY-coordinates of pixels in the image.
- A "mask" that shows which pixels within the bounding box are part of the object. Using the mask data, you can find the outline of the object.

Below is the Python code for detecting the bounding box for machines using the pre-trained Mask R-CNN and OpenCV models:

```
import nump\' as up

import mrcnn config import mrcnn.utils
from mrcnn.model import ñlaskRCNN from pathli b import Path
```

= The corfi gur ati on that the flask-RCNN librm.' u411 usc. class
ñlaskRCNNCorfi g (mrcnn config Colt g.
    DUE = " coco retr ained model corifi g" EvfAGES PER GPL = 1
    GPL COLNT   1
    h   I CLASSES = 1 + 80= in the COCO dataset there are 80 classes +
    1 background class. DETECTION UHN CONFIDENCE = 0.6

= fi'e filter the list of r ecogniti on results so that on1 \' cars remain. def get
car boxes (boxes class i ds).
    car boxes = Q

    for i box in enumerate (boxes).
        = If the found obj eO is not a car them skip it. if class ids [i] in [3 8
        6].
            car boxes.append (box) return up.array' (car boxes)

= The root direct ox\' of the project. ROOT DIR = Path (".")

= Dir eO w.' for savi rig logs and trained model. ñlODEL DIR = ROOT DIR
." " logs"

* Locd path to the file with trained weights.
COCO ñlODEL PATH = ROOT DIR ." " mask rem coco.h5"

= Dourload COCO dataset if necessary'. if not COCO ñlODEL
PATH.exists Q.
    mrcnn.utils.dourload trained weights (COCO ñlODEL PATH)

= Dir eO w.' with images for processing. EvfAGE DIR = ROOT DIR ."
"images"

= \'i deo file or camera for processing - insert a vd uc of 0 if you want to use a
cam era not a video file. VIDEO SOFF CE   " test images ." parking.m@"

= Create a flask-RCNN model in output mode.
model = ñlaskR WU(mode = " inference" model dir = ñlODEL DIR corifi g
= ñlaskR C UCorifi g Q)

= Dourload the pre-train ed model.
modd. load weights (COCO ñlODEL PATH b\' name = True)

* Locati oxi of parking spaces.
pznked cr boies=hone

```python
# Download the video file for which we want to run recognition.
video_capture = cv2.VideoCapture (VIDEO_SOURCE)

# We loop through each frame.
while video_capture.isOpened ():
    success, frame = video_capture.read ()
    if not success:
        break

    # Convert the image from the BGR color model (used by OpenCV) to RGB.
    rgb_image = frame [:, :, -1]

    # We supply the image of the Mask R-CNN model to get the result.
    results = model.detect ([rgb_image], verbose = 0)

    # Mask R-CNN assumes that we recognize objects in multiple images.
    # We transmitted only one image, so we extract only the first result.
    r = results [0]

    # The variable r now contains recognition results:
    # - r ['rois'] - bounding box for each recognized object.
    # - r ['class_ids'] - identifier (type) of the object.
    # - r ['scores'] - degree of confidence.
    # - r ['masks'] - masks of objects (which gives you their outline).

    # Filter the result to get the scope of the car.
    car_boxes = get_car_boxes (r ['rois'], r ['class_ids'])

    print ("Cars found in frame of video:")

    # Display each frame on the frame.
    for box in car_boxes:
        print ("Car", box)

        y1, x1, y2, x2 = box

        # Draw a frame.
        cv2.rectangle (frame, (x1, y1), (x2, y2), (0, 255, 0), 1)

    # Show the frame on the screen.
    cv2.imshow ('Video', frame)

    # Press 'q' to exit.
    if cv2.waitKey (1) & 0xFF == ord ('q'):
        break

# We clear everything after completion.
video_capture.release ()
cv2.destroyAllWindows ()
```

After running this script, an image with a frame around each detected machine will appear on the screen: Also, the coordinates of each machine will be displayed in the console:

```
Cars found in frame of video:
Car: [492 871 551 961]
Car: [450 819 509 913]
Car: [411 774 470 856]
```

So we learned to recognize cars in the image.

We recognize empty parking spaces

We know the pixel coordinates of each machine. Looking through several consecutive frames, we can quickly determine which of the cars did not move and assume that there are parking spaces. But how to understand that the car left the parking lot?

The problem is that the frames of the machines partially overlap each other:

Therefore, if you imagine that each frame represents a parking space, it may turn out that it is partially occupied by the machine, when in fact it is empty. We need to find a way to measure the degree of intersection of two objects to search only for the "most empty" frames.

We will use a measure called Intersection Over Union (ratio of intersection area to total area) or IoU. IoU can be found by calculating the number of pixels where two objects intersect and divide by the number of pixels occupied by these objects:

So we can understand how the very bounding frame of the car intersects with the frame of the parking space. make it easy to determine if parking is free. If the IoU is low, like 0.15, then the car takes up a small part of the parking space. And if it is high, like 0.6, then this means that the car takes up most of the space and you can't park there.

Since IoU is used quite often in computer vision, it is very likely that the corresponding libraries implement this measure. In our library Mask R-CNN, it is implemented as a function mrcnn.utils.compute_overlaps ().

If we have a list of bounding boxes for parking spaces, you can add a check for the presence of cars in this framework by adding a whole line or two of code:

```
# Filter the result to get the scope of the car.
car_boxes = get_car_boxes (r ['rois'], r ['class_ids'])

# We look how much cars intersect with well-known parking spaces.
overlaps = mrcnn.utils.compute_overlaps (car_boxes, parking_areas)

print (overlaps)
```

The result should look something like this:

```
[
 [1. 0.07040032 0. 0.]
 [0.07040032 1. 0.07673165 0.]
 [0. 0. 0.02332112 0.]
]
```

In this two-dimensional array, each row reflects one frame of the parking space. And each column indicates how strongly each of the places intersects with one of the detected machines. A result of 1.0 means that the entire space is entirely occupied by the car, and a low value like 0.02 indicates that the car has climbed into place a little, but you can still park on it.

To find unoccupied places, you just need to check each row in this array. If all numbers are close to zero, then most likely, the place is free!

However, keep in mind that object recognition does not always work correctly with real-time video. Although the model based on Mask R-CNN is wholly accurate, from time to time, it may miss a car or two in one frame of the video. Therefore, before asserting that the place is free, you need to make sure that it remains so for the next 5-10 next frames of video. This way, we can avoid situations when the system mistakenly marks a place empty due to a glitch in one frame of the video. As soon as we make sure that the place remains free for several frames, you can send a message!

Send SMS

The last part of our conveyor is sending SMS notifications when a free parking space appears.

Sending a message from Python is very easy if you use Twilio. Twilio is an accessible API that allows you to send SMS from almost any programming language with just a few lines of code. Of course, if you prefer a different service, you can use it. I have nothing to do with Twilio: it's just the first thing that come to brain .

To using Twilio, sign-up for a trial account, create a Twilio phone number, and get your account authentication information. Then install the client library:

```
$ pip3 install twilio
```

After that, use the following code to send the message:

```python
from twilio.rest import Client

# Twilio account details.
twilio_account_sid = 'Your Twilio SID'
twilio_auth_token = 'Your Twilio Authentication Token'
twilio_source_phone_number = 'Your Twilio Phone Number'

# Create a Twilio client object.
client = Client (twilio_account_sid, twilio_auth_token)

# Send SMS.
message = client.messages.create (
    body = 'Message body',
    from_ = twilio_source_phone_number,
    to = "Your number where the message will come"
)
```

To add the ability to send messages to our script, just copy this code there. However, you need make sure that the message is not sent on every frame, where you can see the free space. Therefore, we will have a flag that in the installed state will not allow sending messages for some time or until another place is vacated.

Putting it all together

```python
import numpy as np
import cv2
import mrcnn.config
import mrcnn.utils
```

```python
from mrcnn.model import MaskRCNN
from pathlib import Path
from twilio.rest import Client

# The configuration that the Mask-RCNN library will use.
class MaskRCNNConfig (mrcnn.config.Config):
    NAME = "coco_pretrained_model_config"
    IMAGES_PER_GPU = 1
    GPU_COUNT = 1
    NUM_CLASSES = 1 + 80 # in the COCO dataset there are 80 classes + 1 background class.
    DETECTION_MIN_CONFIDENCE = 0.6

# We filter the list of recognition results so that only cars remain.
def get_car_boxes (boxes, class_ids):
    car_boxes = []

    for i, box in enumerate (boxes):
        # If the found object is not a car, then skip it.
        if class_ids [i] in [3, 8, 6]:
            car_boxes.append (box)

    return np.array (car_boxes)

# Twilio configuration
twilio_account_sid = 'Your Twilio SID'
twilio_auth_token = 'Your Twilio Authentication Token'
twilio_phone_number = 'Your Twilio Phone Number'
destination_phone_number = 'Number where the message will come'
client = Client (twilio_account_sid, twilio_auth_token)

# The root directory of the project.
ROOT_DIR = Path (".")

# Directory for saving logs and trained model.
MODEL_DIR = ROOT_DIR / "logs"

# Local path to the file with trained weights.
COCO_MODEL_PATH = ROOT_DIR / "mask_rcnn_coco.h5"

# Download COCO dataset if necessary.
if not COCO_MODEL_PATH.exists ():
    mrcnn.utils.download_trained_weights (COCO_MODEL_PATH)

# Directory with images for processing
IMAGE_DIR = ROOT_DIR / "images"

# Video file or camera for processing - insert the value 0 if using a camera, not a video file.
VIDEO_SOURCE = "test_images / parking.mp4"

# Create a Mask-RCNN model in output mode.
model = MaskRCNN (mode = "inference", model_dir = MODEL_DIR, config = MaskRCNNConfig ())

# Download the pre-trained model.
model.load_weights (COCO_MODEL_PATH, by_name = True)
```

Location of parking spaces.

```
parked_car_boxes= None

    Douml oad the st deo file for vhlch ve vant t D run recDgM ti or.
video_capture = eve.\'ideoCapture /fiDE O_S OURCE)

.=. How' mans' frames in a row' math an mnpR.' place we have already' seen.
free space frames = 0

.=. Have w'e d ready sent SMS?
sms sent = Fd se

    "e l cop thfDugh each frame.
whil e s4 deD Capture.isOpened 0
    success, frame = video_capture.read ()
    if not success:
        break

        Corivert the image from the BGR col or model to RGB .
    rgb_ mage = frame [.... .: − I]

    # fi'e supply' the image of the flask R—Ch   model to get the result.
    results = mDdel.detect ([r gb image], s erbDse = 0)

        flask R-CA assumes that 'e recognize  objects in multiple images.
= fi'e tr aris iitted onl>' one imag e, sD we extract Ofll\' the fir st result.
    r = results [0]

= The variable r now' contains recogniti on results.
    =- r rois'] - bounding box for each recognized object:
        - r class ids'] - identifier (type) of the object:
        - r § scar est - degree Df cDn 1 dence:
= - r  masks   masks of objects ( 'hich gi yes von their outline).

    if parked car boxes i s None:
        = Thi s is the first frame Df the videD - let's say' that all detected cars are in the parking l ot.
        = Save the locad on of each car as a parking space and move on tD the next fratne.
        parked_car_boxes = get_car_boxes (• L•ois'], r cl ass_i ds'])
    else:
        = XVe dread>' knor' where the places are. Check if there are an>'.

        = U'e ar e l DDki fly for KOf.S Dn the oirr aut fram e.
        car_boxes = get_car_boxes (r ['rɑ sd .  L+       '])

            1'e 1 Dok hDT' rauch these cars I ntersect a'tth 'ell -knDTW parking
        DS'erl aps = rarcnn.utils.co tpute_a'erl aps {parked_car_bDxes, car_boxes)

        = XVe assume that there are no emph.' seats until 'e find at l east one.
        free_space = Fal se

        = XVe go through the cycle for each well-known parking space.
        fa parking_area. overl ap_areas in zip (parked_car_boxes. overl aps):


            = fi'e are lDDkiflg for the maximum seal ue of the intersectiDH Flth an>' detected
                Dn the frame b5' the machine (no matter w'hich).
            max_I oU_overl ap = up.max (overlap_areas)
```

```python
# We get the upper left and lower right coordinates of the parking space.
    y1, x1, y2, x2 = parking_area

        # Check if space is free by checking the IoU value.
        if max_IoU_overlap < 0.15:
            # Place is free! Draw a green frame around it.
            cv2.rectangle (frame, (x1, y1), (x2, y2), (0, 255, 0), 3)
            # We note that we found at least it is free space
            free_space = True
        else:
            # The place is still taken - we draw a red frame.
            cv2.rectangle (frame, (x1, y1), (x2, y2), (0, 0, 255), 1)

        # Write the IoU value inside the frame.
        font = cv2.FONT_HERSHEY_DUPLEX
        cv2.putText (frame, f" {max_IoU_overlap: 0.2}", (x1 + 6, y2 - 6), font, 0.3, (255, 255, 255))

    # If at least one place was free, we begin to count frames.
    # This is to make sure that the place is really free
    # and do not send another notification.
    if free_space:
        free_space_frames += 1
    else:
        # If everything is busy, reset the counter
        free_space_frames = 0

    # If the place is free for several frames, we can say that it is free.
    if free_space_frames > 10:
        # Display SPACE AVAILABLE !! at the top of the screen.
        font = cv2.FONT_HERSHEY_DUPLEX
        cv2.putText (frame, f"SPACE AVAILABLE!", (10, 150), font, 3.0, (0, 255, 0), 2, cv2.FILLED)

        # Send a message if you have not done so already.
        if not sms_sent:
            print ("SENDING SMS !!!")
            message = client.messages.create (
                body = "Parking space open - go go go!",
                from_ = twilio_phone_number,
                to = destination_phone_number
            )
            sms_sent = True

    # Show the frame on the screen.
    cv2.imshow ('Video', frame)

    # Press 'q' to exit.
    if cv2.waitKey (1) & 0xFF == ord ('q'):
        break

# Press 'q' to exit.
video_capture.release ()
cv2.destroyAllWindows ()
```

To run that code, you first need to install Python 3.6+, Matterport Mask R-CNN, and OpenCV.

I specifically wrote the code as simple as possible. For example, if he sees in the first frame of the car, he concludes that they are all parked. Try experiment with it and see if you can improve its reliability.

Just by changing the identifiers of the objects that the model is looking for, you can turn the code into something completely different. For example, imagine that you are working at a ski resort. After making a couple of changes, you can turn this script into a system that automatically recognizes snowboarders jumping from a ramp and records videos with cool jumps. Or, if you work in a nature reserve, you can create a system that counts zebras. You are limited only by your imagination.

7. CREATING GAMES ON THE PYGAME FRAMEWORK | PART 1

Hi, Python lover!

This is the first of a third-part tutorial on creating games using Python 3 and Pygame. In the second part, we examined the class TextObjec-tused to render text to the screen is created to the main window, and learned how to draw objects: bricks, ball, and racket.

In this part, we will the dive deeper into the heart of Breakout, and learn how to handle events, get acquainted with the main Breakout class, and see how to move various objects in the game.

Event handling

Breakout has three types of events: keystroke events, mouse events, and timer events. The main loop in the Game class handles keystrokes and mouse events and passes them to subscribers (by calling a handler function).

Although the Game class is very general and does not have knowledge about Breakout implementation, the subscription and event handling methods are very specific.

Breakout class

The Breakout class implements most of the knowledge about how Breakout is controlled. In this tutorial series, we will meet the Brea-kout class several times. Here are the lines that various event handlers register.

It should be noted that all key events (for both the left and right "arrows") are transmitted to one racket handler method.

```
# Register the handle_mouse_event () method of the button object
self.mouse_handlers.append (b.handle_mouse_event)

# Register racket handle () method for handling key events
self.keydown_handlers [pygame.K_LEFT] .append (paddle.handle)
self.keydown_handlers [pygame.K_RIGHT] .append (paddle.handle)
self.keyup_handlers [pygame.K_LEFT] .append (paddle.handle)
self.keyup_handlers [pygame.K_RIGHT] .append (paddle.handle)
```

Keystroke handling

The Game class calls registered handlers for each key event and passes the key. Note that this is not a Paddle

class. Into Breakout, the only object that is interested in such events is a racket. When you press or release a key, its method is handle()called. The Paddle object does not need to know if this was a key press or release event, because it controls the current state using a pair of Boolean variables: moving_left and moving_right. If moving_left True, it means that the "left" key was pressed, and the next event will be the release of the key, which will reset the variable. The same applies to the right key. The logic is simple and consists of switching the state of these variables in response to any event.

```
def handle (self, key):
    if key == pygame.K_LEFT:
        self.moving_left = not self.moving_left
    else:
        self.moving_right = not self.moving_right
```

Mouse event handling

Breakout has a game menu that we will meet soon. The menu button controls various mouse events, such as movement and button presses (mouse down and mouse up events). In the response to these events, the button updates the internal state variable. Here is the mouse processing code:

```
def handle_mouse_event (self, type, pos):
    if type == pygame.MOUSEMOTION:
        self.handle_mouse_move (pos)
    elif type == pygame.MOUSEBUTTONDOWN:
        self.handle_mouse_down (pos)
    elif type == pygame.MOUSEBUTTONUP:
        self.handle_mouse_up (pos)

def handle_mouse_move (self, pos):
    if self.bounds.collidepoint (pos):
        if self.state! = 'pressed':
            self.state = 'hover'
    else:
        self.state = 'normal'

def handle_mouse_down (self, pos):
    if self.bounds.collidepoint (pos):
        self.state = 'pressed'

def handle_mouse_up (self, pos):
    if self.state == 'pressed':
        self.on_click (self)
        self.state = 'hover'
```

Notice that the method handle_mouse_event() registered to receive mouse events checks the type of event and redirects it to the appropriate method that processes this type of event.

Handling Timer Events

Timer events are not processed in the main loop. However, since the main loop is called in each frame, it is easy to check whether the time has come for a particular event. You will see this later when we discuss temporary special effects.

Another situation is the need to pause the game. For example, when displaying a message that the player must read and so that nothing distracts him. The show_message()Breakout class method takes this approach and to calls time.sleep(). Here is the relevant code:

```
import config as c

class Breakout (Game):
    def show_message (self,
            text
            color = colors.WHITE,
            font_name = 'Arial',
            font_size = 20,
            centralized = False):
        message = TextObject (c.screen_width // 2,
                c.screen_height // 2,
                lambda: text, color,
                font_name, font_size)
        self.draw ()
        message.draw (self.surface, centralized)
        pygame.display.update ()
        time.sleep (c.message_duration)
```

Game process

Gameplay (gameplay) is where the Breakout rules come into play. The gameplay consists in moving various objects in response to events and in changing the state of the game based on their interactions.

Moving racket

You saw earlier that the Paddle class responds to arrow keys by updating its

fields *moving_left* and *moving_right*. The movement itself occurs in a method *update()*. Certain calculations are performed here if the racket is close to the left or right edge of the screen. We do not want the racket to go beyond the boundaries of the screen (taking into account a given offset).

Therefore, if the movement moves the object beyond the borders, then the code adjusts the movement so that it stops right at the border. Since the racket only moves horizontally to the vertical component of the movement is always zero.

```
import pygame

import config as c
from game_object import GameObject


class Paddle (GameObject):
    def __init__ (self, x, y, w, h, color, offset):
        GameObject.__init__ (self, x, y, w, h)
        self.color = color
        self.offset = offset
        self.moving_left = False
        self.moving_right = False



    def update (self):
        if self.moving_left:
            dx = - (min (self.offset, self.left))
        elif self.moving_right:
            dx = min (self.offset, c.screen_width - self.right)
        else:
            return

        self.move (dx, 0)
```

Moving ball

The ball simply uses the functionality of the base class GameObject, which moves objects based on their speed (its horizontal and vertical components). As we will soon see, the speed of a ball is determined by many factors in the Breakout class. Since the movement consists simply of adding speed to the current position, the direction in which the ball moves is completely determined by the speed along the horizontal and vertical axes.

Setting the initial speed of the ball

The Breakout ball comes out of nowhere at the very beginning of the game every time a player loses his life. It simply materializes from the ether and begins to fall either exactly down or at a slight angle. When the ball is created in the method create_ball(), it gets the speed with a random horizontal component in the range from - 2 to 2 and the vertical component specified in the config.py module (the default value is 3).

```
def create_ball (self):
    speed = (random.randint (-2, 2), c.ball_speed)
    self.ball = Ball (c.screen_width // 2,
                c.screen_height // 2,
                c.ball_radius,
                c.ball_color,
                speed)
    self.objects.append (self.ball)
```

Summarize

In this part, we looked at handling events such as keystrokes, mouse movements, and mouse clicks. We also examined some elements of Breakout gameplay: moving the racket, moving the ball, and controlling the speed of the ball.

In the fourth part, we will consider the important topic of collision recognition and see what happens when the ball hits different game objects: a racket, bricks, walls, ceiling, and floor. Then we will pay attention to the game menu. We will create our buttons, which we use as a menu, and will be able to show and hide if necessary.

Creating games on the Pygame framework | Part 2

This is the Second of a Thired-part tutorial on the creating games using Python 3 and Pygame. In the third part, we delved to the heart of Breakout, and learned how to handle events, got acquainted within the main Breakout class and saw how to move different game objects.

In this part, we will learn the how to recognize collisions and what happens to when a ball hits different object: a racket, bricks, walls, ceiling, and floor. Finally, we will look at the important topic of the user interface, and in particular, how to create the menu from your buttons.

Collision Recognition

In games, the objects collide with each other, and Breakout is no exception. The ball is collides with objects. The main method handle_ball_collisions()has a built-in function is called intersect()that is used to the check whether the ball hit the object and where it collided with the object. It returns 'left,' 'right,' 'top,' 'bottom,' or None if the ball does not collide with an object.

```
def handle_ball_collisions (self):
    def intersect (obj, ball):
        edges = dict (
        left = Rect (obj.left, obj.top, 1, obj.height),
        right = Rect (obj.right, obj.top, 1, obj.height),
        top = Rect (obj.left, obj.top, obj.width, 1),
        bottom = Rect (obj.left, obj.bottom, obj.width, 1))
        collisions = set (edge for edge, rect in edges.items () if
            ball.bounds.collide.rect (rect))
        if not collisions:
            return none

        if len (collisions) == 1:
            return list (collisions) [0]

        if 'top' in collisions:
            if ball.center.y> = obj.top:
                return 'top'
            if ball.center.x <obj.left:
                return 'left'
            else:
                return 'right'

        if 'bottom' in collisions:
            if ball.center.y> = obj.bottom:
                return 'bottom'
            if ball.center.x <obj.left:
                return 'left'
            else:
                return 'right'
```

Collision of a ball with a racket.

When the ball hit the racket, it bounces. If it hit the top of the racket, it bounces back up, but retains same components horizontal fast speed.

But if he hit the side of the racket, it bounces to the opposite side (right or left) and continues to move down until it hits the floor. The code uses a function intersect().

```
# Kick on the racket
s = self.ball.speed
edge = intersect (self.paddle, self.ball)
if edge is not None:
    self.sound_effects ['paddle_hit'].play ()
if edge == 'top':
    speed_x = s [0]
    speed_y = -s [1]
    if self.paddle.moving_left:
        speed_x -= 1
    elif self.paddle.moving_left:
        speed_x += 1
    self.ball.speed = speed_x, speed_y
elif edge in ('left', 'right'):
    self.ball.speed = (-s [0], s [1])
```

Collision with the floor.

The ball hits to the racket from the side, the ball continues fall and then hits the floor. At this moment, the player to loses his life and the ball is recreated so that game can continue. The game ends when player runs out of life.

```
# Hit the floor
if self.ball.top > c.screen_height:
    self.lives -= 1
    if self.lives == 0:
        self.game_over = True
    else:
        self.create_ball ()
```

Collision with ceiling and walls

When a ball hits the wall or ceiling, it simply bounces off them.

```
# Hit the ceiling
if self.ball.top <0:
    self.ball.speed = (s [0], -s [1])

# Kick against the wall
if self.ball.left <0 or self.ball.right> c.screen_width:
    self.ball.speed = (-s [0], s [1])
```

Collision with bricks

When ball hits a brick, this is the main event the Breakout game - the brick disappeared, the player receives a point, the ball bounce back, and several more events occur (sound effect, and sometimes a special effect), which we will consider later.

To determine that the ball has hit a brick, the code will check if any of the bricks intersects with the ball:

```
#Bump on a brick
for brick in self.bricks:
    edge = intersect (brick, self.ball)
    if not edge:
        continue

self.bricks.remove (brick)
self.objects.remove (brick)
self.score + = self.points_per_brick

if edge in ('top', 'bottom'):
    self.ball.speed = (s [0], -s [1])
else:
    self.ball.speed = (-s [0], s [1])
```

Game Menu Design Program

Most games have some kind of U.I. Breakout has simple menu with two buttons, 'PLAY' and 'QUIT.' The menu is display at the beginning of the game and disappears when the player clicks on 'PLAY.'

Let's see how the button and menu are implemented, as well as how they integrate into the game.

Button Creation

Pygame has no built-in UI library. The third-party extensions, but for the menu, we decided to create our buttons. that has three states: normal, highlighted, and press. The normal state when the mouse is not above the buttons, and the highlight state is when the mouse is above the button, the left mouse button not yet press. The press state is when the mouse is above the button, and the player pressed the left mouse button.

The buttons implement as a rectangle with a back ground color and text display on top of it. The button also receive the (onclick function), which is called when the button is clicked.

```python
import pygame

from game_object import GameObject
from text_object import TextObject
import config as c


class Button (GameObject):
    def __init__(self,
                 x,
                 y,
                 w,
                 h,
                 text,
                 on_click = lambda x: None,
                 padding = 0):
        super().__init__(x, y, w, h)
        self.state = 'normal'
        self.on_click = on_click

        self.text = TextObject(x + padding,
                               y + padding, lambda: text,
                               c.button_text_color,
                               c.font_name,
                               c.font_size)

    def draw(self, surface):
        pygame.draw.rect(surface,
                         self.back_color,
                         self.bounds)
        self.text.draw(surface)
```

The button process its own mouse events and changes its internal state based on these events. When the button is in the press state and receives the event *MOUSE BUTTONUP*, this means that the player has press the button and the function is called *on _ click()*.

```
def handle_mouse_event (self, type, pos):
    if type == pygame.MOUSEMOTION:
        self.handle_mouse_move (pos)
    elif type == pygame.MOUSEBUTTONDOWN:
        self.handle_mouse_down (pos)
    elif type == pygame.MOUSEBUTTONUP:
        self.handle_mouse_up (pos)

def handle_mouse_move (self, pos):
    if self.bounds.collidepoint (pos):
        if self.state! = 'pressed':
            self.state = 'hover'
    else:
        self.state = 'normal'

def handle_mouse_down (self, pos):
    if self.bounds.collidepoint (pos):
        self.state = 'pressed'

def handle_mouse_up (self, pos):
    if self.state == 'pressed':
        self.on_click (self)
        self.state = 'hover'
```

The property *back _ color* used to draw on the background rectangle to always returns the color corresponding to current form of the button, so that it is clear to the player that the button is active:

```
@property
def back_color (self):
    return dict (normal = c.button_normal_back_color,
        hover = c.button_hover_back_color,
        pressed = c.button_pressed_back_color) [self.state]
```

Menu Design

The function *create_menu()* create a menu with two buttons with the text 'PLAY' and 'QUIT.' It has two built- in function, *on _ play* ()and *on _ quit* ()which it pass to the correspond button. Each button is add to the list *objects* (for rendering), as well as in the field *menu _ buttons*.

```
def create_menu (self):
    for i, (text, handler) in enumerate ((('PLAY', on_play),
                                          ('QUIT', on_quit))):
        b = Button (c.menu_offset_x,
            c.menu_offset_y + (c.menu_button_h + 5) * i,
            c.menu_button_w,
            c.menu_button_h,
            text,
            handler
            padding = 5)
        self.objects.append (b)
        self.menu_buttons.append (b)
        self.mouse_handlers.append (b.handle_mouse_event)
```

When PLAY the button is prese *onplay()*, a function is called that removes the button from the list *object* so that the no longer drawn. In adding, the values of the Boolean field that trigger the starting of the game - *is_gamerunningandstartlevel*-Thats OK

When the button is press, QUIT is _ game_ runningtakes on value (False)(in fact, pausing the game), it set game_ over to True, which triggers the sequence of completion of the game.

```
def on_play (button):
    for b in self.menu_buttons:
    self.objects.remove (b)

    self.is_game_running = True
    self.start_level = True

    def on_quit (button):
    self.game_over = True
    self.is_game_running = False
```

Show and hide GameMenu

The display and hiding the menu are performed implicitly. When the buttons are in the list object, the menu is visible : when they removed, it is hidden. Everything is very simple.

Create built-in menu with its surface that renders its subcomponents (buttons and other objects) and then simply add or remove these menu components, but this is not required for such a simple menu.

To summarize

We examined the collision recognition and what happens when the ball collides with the different objects: a racket, bricks, walls, floor, and ceiling. We also created a menu with our buttons, which can be hidden and displayed on command.

In last part of the series, we will consider completion of the game, tracking points, and lives, sound effects, and music.

We develop complex system of special effects that add few spices to game. Finally, we will the discuss further development and possible improvements.

Creating games on the Pygame framework| Part 3

This is the last of the Thired parts of the tutorial on creating games using Python 3 and PyGame. In the fourth part, we learned to recognize collisions, respond to the fact that the ball collides with different game objects, and created a game menu with its buttons.

In last part, we will look at various topics: the end of the game, managing lives and points, sound effects, music, and even a flexible system of special effects. For dessert, we will consider possible improvements and directions for further development.

End of the game

Sooner or later, the game should end. In this form of Breakout, the game ends in one of two ways: the player either loses all his life or destroys all the bricks. There is no next level in the game (but it can easily be added).

Game over!

The game_overclass of the Game class is set to False in the method init()of the Game class. The main loop continues until the variable game_overchanges to True :

```
class Game:
    def __init__ (self,
                  caption
                  width
                  height
                  back_image_filename,
                  frame_rate):

        self.game_over = False


def run (self):
    while not self.game_over:
        self.surface.blit (self.background_image, (0, 0))

        self.handle_events ()
        self.update ()
        self.draw ()

        pygame.display.update ()
        self.clock.tick (self.frame_rate)
```

All this happens in the Breakout class in the following cases:

- The player presses the QUIT button in the menu.
- The player loses his last life.
- The player destroys all bricks.

```
def on_quit (button):
    self.game_over = True
    self.is_game_running = False

def handle_ball_collisions (self):

    # Hit the floor
    if self.ball.top > c.screen_height:
        self.lives -= 1
        if self.lives == 0:
            self.game_over = True

            if not self.bricks:
                self.show_message ('YOU WIN !!!', centralized = True)
                self.is_game_running = False
                self.game_over = True
                return

def update (self):

    if not self.bricks:
        self.show_message ('YOU WIN !!!', centralized = True)
        self.is_game_running = False
        self.game_over = True
        return
```

Game End Message Display

Usually, at the end of the game, we do not want the game window to disappear silently. An exception is a case when we click on the QUIT button in the menu. When a player loses their last life, Breakout displays the traditional message 'GAME OVER!', And when the player wins, it shows the message 'YOU WIN!'

In both cases, the function is used show_message(). It displays text on top of the current screen (the game pauses) and waits a few seconds to before returning. The next iteration of the game loop, checking the field game_overwill determine that it is True, after which the program will end.

This is what the function looks like show_message():

```
def show_message (self,
        text,
        color = colors.WHITE,
        font_name = 'Arial',
        font_size = 20,
        centralized = False):
    message = TextObject (c.screen_width // 2,
            c.screen_height // 2,
            lambda: text,
            color,
            font_name,
            font_size)
    self.draw ()
    message.draw (self.surface, centralized)
    pygame.display.update ()
    time.sleep (c.message_duration)
```

Saving records between games

In this version of the game, we do not save records, because there is only one level in it, and the results of all players after the destruction of the bricks will be the same. In general, saving records can be implemented locally, saving records to a file and displaying another message if a player breaks a record.

Adding Sound Effects and Music

Games are an audiovisual process. Many games have sound effects - short audio clips that are played when a player kills monsters finds a treasure, or a terrible death. Some games also have background music that contributes to the atmosphere. There are only sound effects in Breakout, but we will show you how to play music in your games.

Sound effects

To play sound effects, we need sound files (as is the case with image files). These files can be.wav, .mp3, or .ogg format. Breakout stores its sound effects in a folder sound_effects:

```
~/ git / pygame-breakout> tree sound_effects /
sound_effects /
+-- brick_hit.wav
+-- effect_done.wav
+-- level_complete.wav
+-- paddle_hit.wav
```

Let's see how these sound effects load and play at the right time. First, play sound effects (or background music), we need to initialize the Pygame sound system. This is done in the Game class:pygame.mixer.pre_init(44100, 16, 2, 4096)

Then, in the Breakout class, all sound effects are loaded from config into the object pygame mixer Soundand stored in the dictionary:

```
# In config.py
sounds_effects = dict (
    brick_hit = 'sound_effects / brick_hit.wav',
    effect_done = 'sound_effects / effect_done.wav',
    paddle_hit = 'sound_effects / paddle_hit.wav',
    level_complete = 'sound_effects / level_complete.wav',
)

# In breakout.py
class Breakout (Game):
    def __init__ (self):
        ...
        self.sound_effects = {
            name: pygame.mixer.Sound (sound)
            for name, sound in c.sounds_effects.items ()}
        ...
```

Now we can play sound effects when something interesting happens. For example, when a ball hits a brick:

```
#Bump on a brick
for brick in self.bricks:
    edge = intersect (brick, self.ball)
    if not edge:
        continue

self.sound_effects['brick_hit'].play ()
```

The sound effect is played asynchronously: that is, the game does not stop while it is playing. Several sound effects can be played at the same time.

Record your sound effects and messages

Recording your sound effects can be a simple and fun experience. Unlike creating visual resources, it does not require much talent. Anyone can say "Boom!" or "Jump," or shout, "They killed you. Get lucky another time! "

Playing background music

Background music should play continuously. Theoretically, a very long sound effect can be created, but the looped background music is most often used. Music files can be in .wav, .mp3, or .midi format. Here's how the music is implemented:

```
music = pygame.mixer.music.load ('background_music.mp3')
pygame.mixer.music.play (-1, 0.0)
```

Only one background music can play at a time. However, several sound effects can be played on top of background music. This is what is called mixing.

Adding Advanced Features

Let's do something curious. It is interesting to destroy bricks with a ball, but it quickly bothers. What about the overall special effects system? We will develop an extensible special effects system associated with some bricks, which is activated when the ball hits the brick.

This is what the plan will be. Effects have a lifetime. The effect begins when the brick collapses and ends when the effect expires. What happens if the ball hits another brick with a special effect? In theory, you can create compatible effects, but to simplify everything in the original implementation, the active effect will stop, and a new effect will take its place.,

Special effects system

In the most general case, a special effect can be defined as two purposes. The first role activates the effect, and the second reset it. We want attach effects to bricks and give the player a clear understanding of which bricks special , so they can try to hit them or avoid them at certain points.

Our special effects are determined by the dictionary from the module breakout.py. Each effect has a name (for example, long_paddle) and a value that consists of a brick color, as well as two functions. Functions are defined a lambda functions that take a Game instance, which includes everything that can change the special effect in Breakout.

```
special_effects = dict (
    long_paddle = (
        colors.ORANGE,
        lambda g: g.paddle.bounds.inflate_ip (
                c.paddle_width // 2, 0),
        lambda g: g.paddle.bounds.inflate_ip (
                -c.paddle_width // 2, 0)),
    slow_ball = (
        colors.AQUAMARINE2,
        lambda g: g.change_ball_speed (-1),
        lambda g: g.change_ball_speed (1)),
    tripple_points = (
        colors.DARKSEAGREEN4,
        lambda g: g.set_points_per_brick (3),
        lambda g: g.set_points_per_brick (1)),
    extra_life = (
        colors.GOLD1,
        lambda g: g.add_life (),
        lambda g: None))
```

When creating bricks, they can be assigned one of the special effects. Here is the code:

```
def create_bricks (self):
    w = c.brick_width
    h = c.brick_height
    brick_count = c.screen_width // (w + 1)
    offset_x = (c.screen_width - brick_count * (w + 1)) // 2

    bricks = []
    for row in range (c.row_count):
        for col in range (brick_count):
            effect = None
            brick_color = c.brick_color
            index = random.randint (0, 10)
            if index < len (special_effects):
                x = list (special_effects.values ()) [index]
                brick_color = x [0]
                effect = x [1:]

            brick = Brick (offset_x + col * (w + 1),
                    c.offset_y + row * (h + 1),
                    w
                    h
                    brick_color,
                    effect)
            bricks.append (brick)
            self.objects.append (brick)
    self.bricks = bricks
The Brick class has an
```

effect field, which usually has the value None, but (with a probability of 30%) may contain one of the special effects defined above. Note that this code does not know what effects exist. He simply receives the effect and color of the brick and, if necessary, assigns them.

In this version of Breakout, we only trigger effects when we hit a brick, but you can come up with other options for triggering events. The previous effect is discarded (if it existed), and then a new effect is launched. The reset function and effect start time are stored for future use.

```
if brick.special_effect is not None:
    # Reset the previous effect, if any
    if self.reset_effect is not None:
        self.reset_effect (self)

    # Triggering a special effect
    self.effect_start_time = datetime.now ()
    brick.special_effect [0] (self)
    # Setting the current effect reset function
    self.reset_effect = brick.special_effect [1]
```

If the new effect is not launched, we still need to reset the current effect after its lifetime. This happens in the method update(). In each frame, a function to reset the current effect is assigned to the field reset_effect. If the time after starting the current effect exceeds the duration of the effect, then the function is called reset_effect(), and the field reset_effecttakes the value None (meaning that there are currently no active effects).

```
# Reset special effect if necessary
if self.reset_effect:
    elapsed = datetime.now () - self.effect_start_time
    if elapsed> = timedelta (seconds = c.effect_duration):
        self.reset_effect (self)
        self.reset_effect = None
```

Racket increase

The effect of a long racket is to increase the racket by 50%. Its reset function returns the racket to its normal size. The brick has the color Orange.:

```
long_paddle = (
    colors.ORANGE,
    lambda g: g.paddle.bounds.inflate_ip (
        c.paddle_width // 2, 0),
    lambda g: g.paddle.bounds.inflate_ip (
        -c.paddle_width // 2, 0)),
```

Ball slowdown

Another effect that helps in chasing the ball is slowing the ball, that is, reducing its speed by one unit. The brick has an Aquamarine color.

```
slow_ball = (colors.AQUAMARINE2,
    lambda g: g.change_ball_speed (-1),
    lambda g: g.change_ball_speed (1)),
```

More points

If you want great results, then you will like the effect of tripling points, giving three points for each destroyed brick instead of the standard one point. The brick is dark green.

```
tripple_points = (colors.DARKSEAGREEN4,
        lambda g: g.set_points_per_brick (3),
        lambda g: g.set_points_per_brick (1)),
```

Extra lives

Finally, a very useful effect will be the effect of extra lives. He just gives you another life. It does not need a reset. The brick has a gold color.

```
extra_life = (colors.GOLD1,
        lambda g: g.add_life (),
        lambda g: None))
```

Future Features

There are several logical directions for expanding Breakout. If you are interested in trying on yourself in adding new features and functions, here are a few ideas.

Go to the next level

To turn Breakout into a serious game, you need levels: one is not enough. At the beginning of each level, we will reset the screen, but save points and lives. To complicate the game, you can slightly increase the speed of the ball at each level or add another layer of bricks.

Second ball

The effect of temporarily adding a second ball will create enormous chaos. The difficulty here is to treat both balls as equal, regardless of which one is the original. When one ball disappears, the game continues with the only remaining. Life is not lost.

Lasting records

When you have levels with increasing difficulty, it is advisable to create a high score table. You can store records in a file so that they are saved after the game. When a player breaks a record, you can add small pizzas or let him write a name (traditionally with only three characters).

Bombs and bonuses

In the current implementation on, all special effects are associated with bricks, but you can add effects (good and bad) falling from the sky, which the player can collect or avoid.

Summarize

Developing Breakout with Python 3 and Pygame has proven to be an enjoyable experience. This is a compelling combination for creating 2D games (and for 3D games too). If you love Python and want to create your games, then do not hesitate to choose Pygame.

8. OBJECT-ORIENTED PROGRAMMING (OOP) IN PYTHON 3

Algorithms and data structures

Hi, Python lover!

Table of contents

you will become familiars with the following basic concepts of OOP in Python:

- Python Classes
- Object Instances
- Definition and work with methods
- OOP Inheritance

What is object-oriented programming (OOP)?

Object-oriented programming, or, in short, OOP, is a programming paradigm that provides a means of structuring programs in such a way that properties and behavior are combined into separate objects.

For example, an object can represent a person with a name, age, address, etc., with behaviors such as walking, talking, breathing, and running. Or an email with properties such as a recipient list, subject, body, etc., as well as with behaviors such as adding attachments and sending.

In other words, object-oriented programming is an approach for modeling specific real things, such as cars, as well as the relationships between things like companies and employees, students and teachers, etc. OOP models real objects as program objects that have some data that are associated with it and can performs certain function.

Another common program para-digm is procedural program, which structure a program like a recipe in the sense that it provides a set of steps in the form of functions and blocks of code that are executed sequentially to complete a task.

The key conclusion is that objects are at the center of the paradigm of object-oriented programming, representing not only data, as in procedural programming, but also in the general structure of the program.

NOTE Since Python is a programming language with many paradigms, you can choose the paradigm that is best suited to the problem in question, mix different para-digms in one program or switching from one para-digm to another as your program develops.

Python classes

Focusing first on the data, each object or thing is an instance of some class.

The primitive data structures available in Python, such as numbers, strings, and lists, are designed to represent simple things, such as the value of something, the name of the poem, and your favorite colors, respectively.

What if you want to imagine something much more complex?

For example, let say you wanted to track several different animals. If you use a list, the first element may be the name of the animal, while the second element may represent its age.

How would you know which element should be? What if you had 100 different animals? Are you sure that every animal has a name, age, and so on? What if you want to add other properties to these animals? This is not enough organization, and this is exactly what you need for classes.

Classes are used to create new user data structure that contain arbitrary informations abouts some thing. In this case of an animal, we could creates an Animal()class to track animal properties such as name and age.

It is importants to note that a class simply provides structure - it is an example of how something should be defined, but in fact, it does not provide any real content. Animal()The class may indicate that the name and age are required to determine the animal, but it will not claim that the name or age of a particular animal is.

This can help present the class as an idea of how something should be defined.

Python Objects (Instances)

While a class is a plan, an instance is a copy of a class with actual values, literally an object belonging to a particular class. This is no longer an idea: it's a real animal, like a dog named Roger, which is eight years old.

In other words, a class is a form or profile. It determines the necessary informations. After you fullfill out the form, your specific copy is an instance of the class: it contains up-to-date information relevant to you.

You can fill out several copies to create many different copies, but without a form, as a guide, you would be lost without knowing what information is required. Thus, before you can create separate instances of an object, we must first specify what you need by defining a class.

How to define a class in Python

Defining a class is simple in Python:

```
class Dog:
    pass
```

You start with a classkeyword to indicate that you are creating a class, then you add the class name (using theCamelCase notation starting with a capital letter).

Also here we used the Python keyword pass. This is huge often used as a placeholder where the code will eventually go. This allows us to run this code without generating an error.

Note: the above code is correct in Python 3. On Python 2.x ("deprecated Python"), you would use a slightly different class definition:

```
# Python 2.x Class Definition:
class Dog (object):
    pass
```

Not the (object)parts in parentheses indicate the parent class that you are inheriting from (more on this below). In Python-3, this is no longer necessary because it is implicit by defaulting.

Instance attribute

All class create objects, and all objects contain characteristics called attributes (called properties in the first paragraph). Use the init()method to initialize (for example, determine) the initial attributes of an object by giving them a default value (state). This method must have atleast one argument, as well as a self variable that refers to the object itself (for example, Dog).

```
class Dog:

    # Initializer / Instance Attributes
    def __init__(self, name, age):
        self.name = name
        self.age = age
```

In our Dog()class, each dog has a specific name and age, which is certainly important to know when you start creating different dogs. Remember: the class is intended only to define a dog, and not to create instances of individual dogs with specific names and ages: we will come back to this soon.

Similarly, a self variable is also an instance of a class. Since class instances have different meanings, we could argue, Dog.name = namenot self.name = name. But since not all dogs have the same name, we must be able to assign different values for different instances. Hence the need for a special self variable that will help track individual instances of each class.

NOTE: you will never have to call a init()method: it is called automatically when a new instance of Dog is created.

Class attributes

Although instance attributes are specific to each object, class attributes are the same for all instances, in this case, all dogs.

```
class Dog:

    # Class Attribute
    species = 'mammal'

    # Initializer / Instance Attributes
    def __init__(self, name, age):
        self.name = name
        self.age = age
```

Thus, although each dog has a unique name and age, each dog will be a mammal. Let's create some dogs ...

Create Objects

Instantiating is an unusual term for creating a new unique instance of a class.

For example: >>>

```
>>> class Dog:
... pass
...
>>> Dog()
<__main__.Dog object at 0x1004ccc50>
>>> Dog()
<__main__.Dog object at 0x1004ccc90>
>>> a = Dog()
>>> b = Dog()
>>> a == b
False
```

We started by define a new Dog()class, then created two new dogs, each of which was assigned to different

objects. So, to create an instance of the class, you use the class name follow by parentheses. Then, to demonstration that each instance is actually different, we created two more dogs, assigning each variable, and then checking to see if these variables are equal.

What do you think is the type of class instance? >>>

```
>>> class Dog:
... pass
...
>>> a = Dog()
>>> type(a)
<class '__main__.Dog'>
```

Let's look at the more complex example ...

```
class Dog:

    # Class Attribute
    species = 'mammal'

    # Initializer / Instance Attributes
    def __init__(self, name, age):
        self.name = name
        self.age = age


# Instantiate the Dog object
philo = Dog ("Philo", 5)
mikey = Dog ("Mikey", 6)

# Access the instance attributes
print ("{} is {} and {} is {}.".format (
    philo.name, philo.age, mikey.name, mikey.age))

# Is Philo a mammal?
if philo.species == "mammal":
    print (" {0} is a {1}!".format (philo.name, philo.species))
```

NOTE Notice how we use point records to access the attributes of each objects. Save as (dog_class.py), then run program. You should see:

```
Philo is 5 and Mikey is 6.
Philo is a mammal!
```

What's the matter?

We create a new instance of the Dog()class and assigned it to a variable Philo. Then we passed him two arguments, "Philo" and 5, which represent the name and age of this dog, respectively.

These attribute are pass to the init method, which is called every time you creates a new attaching, instance the name and age to the object. You may be wondering why we should not have given self arguments.

This is the magic of Python: when you create a new instance of the class, Python automatically determines what selfies (in this case, Dog), and passes it to the init method.

Review of exercises (# 1)

Exercise: "The oldest dog"

Using the same Dogclass, create three new dogs, each with a different age. Then write a function with a name get_biggest_number()that takes any number of ages (*args) and returns the oldest. Then print the age of the oldest dog something like this:

The oldest dog is 7 years old. Solution: "The oldest dog"   Solution "The oldest dog."

```
class Dog:

    # Class Attribute
    species = 'mammal'

    # Initializer / Instance Attributes
    def __init__(self, name, age):
        self.name = name
        self.age = age


# Instantiate the Dog object
jake = Dog ("Jake", 7)
doug = Dog ("Doug", 4)
william = Dog ("William", 5)


# Determine the oldest dog
def get_biggest_number (* args):
    return max (args)


# Output
print ("The oldest dog is {} years old.".format (
    get_biggest_number (jake.age, doug.age, william.age)))
```

Instance Methods

Instance methods are defined inside the class and are used to get the contents of the instance. They can also be used to perform operation with the attribute of our objects. Like ainit method, the first argument is always self:

```
class Dog:

    # Class Attribute
    species = 'mammal'

    # Initializer / Instance Attributes
    def __init__ (self, name, age):
        self.name = name
        self.age = age

    # instance method
    def description (self):
        return " {} is {} years old" .format (self.name, self.age)

    # instance method
    def speak (self, sound):
        return " {} says {}" . format (self.name, sound)

# Instantiate the Dog object
mikey = Dog ("Mikey", 6)

# call our instance methods
print (mikey.description ())
print (mikey.speak (" Gruff Gruff"))
```

Save as dog_instance_methods.py , then run it:

```
Mikey is 6 years old
Mikey says Gruff Gruff
```

In the last method, speak()we define the behavior. What other types of behavior can you assign to a dog? Go back to the beginning of the paragraph to see examples of the behavior of other objects.

Attribute Change

You can changes the value of attributes based on some behavior: >>>

```
>>> class Email:
... def __init__ (self):
... self.is_sent = False
... def send_email (self):
... self.is_sent = True
...
>>> my_email = Email ()
>>> my_email.is_sent
False
>>> my_email.send_email ()
>>> my_email.is_sent
True
```

Here we added a method for sending an email that updates the is_sentvariable to True.

Python object inheritance

Inheritance is a processing in which one class accepts the attributes and methods of another. Newly created classes are called child classes, and the classes from which the child classes derive are called parent classes.

It is importants to note that child classes override or extend the functionality (for example, attributes and behavior) of parent classes. In other words, child classes inherit all the attributes and behavior of the parent, but can also define other behavior to be followed. The most basic type of class is the class object, which usually all other classes inherit as the parents.

When you defining a new class, Python 3 implicitly uses its object as the parent class. Thus, the following two definitions are equivalent:

```python
class Dog (object):
    pass

# In Python 3, this is the same as:

class Dog:
    pass
```

Note. In Python 2.x, there is a difference between the new and old-style classes. I will not go into details, but you will usually want to specify an object as the parent class to make sure that you define a new style class if you are writing Python 2 OOP code.

Dog Park Example

Let's imagine that we are in a dog park. There are several Dog objects involved in Dog behavior, each with different attributes. In ordinary conversation, this means that some dogs are running, and some are stretched, and some are just watching other dogs. Besides, each dog was named its owner, and since each dog lives and breathes, each is aging.

How else can you distinguish one dog from another? How about a dog breed:>>>

```
>>> class Dog
... def __init__ (self, breed):
... self.breed = breed
...
>>> spencer = Dog ("German Shepard")
>>> spencer.breed
'German Shepard'
>>> sara = Dog ("Boston Terrier")
>>> sara.breed
'Boston Terrier'
```

Each dog breed has slightly different behaviors. To take this into account, let's create separate classes for each breed. These are child classes of the parent Dogclass.

Extending parent class functionality

Create new file this called dog_inheritance.py :

```python
# Parent class
class Dog:

    # Class attribute
    species = 'mammal'

    # Initializer / Instance attributes
    def __init__(self, name, age):
        self.name = name
        self.age = age

    # instance method
    def description(self):
        return "{} is {} years old".format(self.name, self.age)

    # instance method
    def speak(self, sound):
        return "{} says {}".format(self.name, sound)


# Child class (inherits from Dog class)
class RussellTerrier(Dog):
    def run(self, speed):
        return "{} runs {}".format(self.name, speed)

# Child class (inherits from Dog class)
class Bulldog(Dog):
    def run(self, speed):
        return "{} runs {}".format(self.name, speed)


# Child classes inherit attributes and
# behaviors from the parent class
jim = Bulldog("Jim", 12)
print(jim.description())

# Child classes have specific attributes
# and behaviors as well
print(jim.run("slowly"))
```

Read the comments aloud while you are working with this program to help you understand what is happening, and then, before you run the program, see if you can predict the expected result.

You should see:

```
Jim is 12 years old
Jim runs slowly
```

We did not add any special attributes or methods to distinguish between a RussellTerrierand a Bulldog. Still, since they are now two different classes, we could, for example, give them different class attributes that determine their respective speeds.

Parent and child classes

isinstance()The function is used to determine if the instance is also an instance of a specific parent class. Save this as dog_isinstance.py :

```python
# Parent class
class Dog:

    # Class attribute
    species = 'mammal'

    # Initializer / Instance attributes
    def __init__(self, name, age):
        self.name = name
        self.age = age

    # instance method
    def description(self):
        return "{} is {} years old".format(self.name, self.age)

    # instance method
    def speak(self, sound):
        return "{} says {}".format(self.name, sound)

# Child class (inherits from Dog () class)
class RussellTerrier(Dog):
    def run(self, speed):
        return "{} runs {}".format(self.name, speed)

# Child class (inherits from Dog () class)
class Bulldog(Dog):
    def run(self, speed):
        return "{} runs {}".format(self.name, speed)


# Child classes inherit attributes and
# behaviors from the parent class
jim = Bulldog("Jim", 12)
print(jim.description())

# Child classes have specific attributes
# and behaviors as well
print(jim.run("slowly"))

# Is jim an instance of Dog ()?
print(isinstance(jim, Dog))

# Is julie an instance of Dog ()?
julie = Dog("Julie", 100)
print(isinstance(julie, Dog))

# Is johnny walker an instance of Bulldog ()
johnnywalker = RussellTerrier("Johnny Walker", 4)
print(isinstance(johnnywalker, Bulldog))

# Is julie and instance of jim?
print(isinstance(julie, jim))
```

Conclusion: >>>

```
('Jim', 12)
Jim runs slowly
True
True
False
Traceback (most recent call last):
  File "dog_isinstance.py", line 50, in <module>
    print (isinstance (julie, jim))
TypeError: isinstance () arg 2 must be a class, type, or tuple of classes and types
```

It makes sense? Both jimandjulieare instances of the Dog()class and johnnywalkerare not instances of Bulldog()the class. Then, as a health check, we checked juliewhether the instance is an instance jim, which is impossible, since jimitinstancedoes not belong to the class itself, but to the class TypeError.

Overriding parent class functionality

Remember that child classes can also override the attributes and behavior of the parent class. For example: >>>

```
>>> class Dog:
... species = 'mammal'
...
>>> class SomeBreed (Dog):
... pass
...
>>> class SomeOtherBreed (Dog):
... species = 'reptile'
...
>>> frank = SomeBreed ()
>>> frank.species 'mammal'
>>> beans = SomeOtherBreed ()
>>> beans.species 'reptile'
```
The SomeBreed()class inherits speciesfrom the parent class, while the SomeOtherBreed()class overrides speciesby setting it reptile.

Review of exercises (# 2)

Exercise: "Legacy of the dogs"

Create a Petsclass that contains dog instances: this class is completely separate from the Dogclass. In other words, a Dogclass is not inherited from the Petsclass. Then assign three instances of the dog to the Petsclassinstance . Start with the following code below. Save the file as pets_class.py . Your output should look like this:

```
I have 3 dogs.
Tom is 6.
Fletcher is 7.
Larry is 9.
And they're all mammals, of course.
```

Start Code:

```
# Parent class
class Dog:

    # Class attribute
    species = 'mammal'

    # Initializer / Instance attributes
    def __init__(self, name, age):
        self.name = name
        self.age = age

    # instance method
    def description(self):
        return '{} is {} years old'.format(self.name, self.age)

    # instance method
    def speak(self, sound):
        return '{} says {}'.format(self.name, sound)

# Child class (inherits from Dog class)
class RussellTerrier(Dog):
    def run(self, speed):
        return '{} runs {}'.format(self.name, speed)

# Child class (inherits from Dog class)
class Bulldog(Dog):
    def run(self, speed):
        return '{} runs {}'.format(self.name, speed)
```

Solution: "Dog Inheritance"

```python
# Parent class
class Pets:

    dogs = []

    def __init__(self, dogs):
        self.dogs = dogs


# Parent class
class Dog:

    # Class attribute
    species = 'mammal'

    # Initializer / Instance attributes
    def __init__(self, name, age):
        self.name = name
        self.age = age

    # Instance method
    def description(self):
        return self.name, self.age

    # Instance method
    def speak(self, sound):
        return "% s says% s" % (self.name, sound)

    # Instance method
    def eat(self):
        self.is_hungry = False


# Child class (inherits from Dog class)
class RussellTerrier(Dog):
    def run(self, speed):
        return "% s runs% s" % (self.name, speed)


# Child class (inherits from Dog class)
class Bulldog(Dog):
    def run(self, speed):
        return "% s runs% s" % (self.name, speed)

# Create instances of dogs
my_dogs = [
    Bulldog("Tom", 6),
    RussellTerrier("Fletcher", 7),
    Dog("Larry", 9)
]

# Instantiate the Pets class
my_pets = Pets(my_dogs)

# Output
print("I have {} dogs.".format(len(my_pets.dogs)))
for dog in my_pets.dogs:
    print("  {} is {}.".format(dog.name, dog.age))

print("And they're all {} s, of course.".format(dog.species))
```

Exercise: Hungry Dogs

Use the same files, add an instance attribute is_hungry = Truein the Dogclass. Then add the called method, eat()which when called changes the value is_hungryto False. Find out how best to feed each dog, and then print "My dogs are hungry." if everyone is hungry or "My dogs are not hungry." if everyone is not hungry. The final result should look like this:

```
I have 3 dogs.
Tom is 6.
Fletcher is 7.
Larry is 9.
And they're all mammals, of course.
My dogs are not hungry.
```

Solution: Hungry Dogs

```
# Parent class
class Pets:

    dogs = []

    def __init__(self, dogs):
        self.dogs = dogs

# Parent class

class Dog:

    * Class attribute
    speed es = 'mamm d'

    * Initi d i zer." In stance attributes
    def iriit (self name age):
        self.name  = name
        self.age  = age
        self.is hungo.' = True

    = mist ance method
    def descripti on (self):
        return self.name self.age

    = mist ance method
    def speak (self sound):
        return " °. o s says°. o s" °. o (self.name sound)
```

```
= mist ance method
    def eat (self).
        self.is hungo.' = Fdse


= Oiild class (inherits from Dog cl ass)
class RussellT erri er (Dog).
    def run (self speed).
        return " °. o s runs°. o s" °. o (self.name speedt


= Oiild class (inherits from Dog cl ass)
class Bulldog (Dog.
    def run (self speed).
        return " °. o s runs°. o s" °. o (self.name speedt

= Create instances of dogs
m\' dogs = [
    Bulldog (" Tom" 6)
    Ru ssellT erri er (" FI ct cher" Ti
    Dog ("L are.'" 9)


    stanttate the Pets class
ate'   ts = Pets (ate' dogs)

= Output
print (" I h ave { ) dogs.". format (len (m\'   ets.dogs)))
for dog in m\'   ets.dogs.
    dog.eat Q
    print (" { ) is { ).". format (dog.name dog.age))

print ("And the\''re d1 { ) s of ccxirse." . format (dog.species))

are m\' dogs hungo.' = Fdse
for dog in m\'   ets.dogs.
    if dog.i s hungo.'.
```

```
are_my_dogs_hungry = True

if are_my_dogs_hungry:
    print ('My dogs are hungry.')
else:
    print ('My dogs are not hungry.')
```

Exercise: "Dog Walking"

Next, add a walk()method like PetsandDogclasses, so that when you call a method in the Petsclass, each instance of a dog is assigned to Petsa class walk(). Save this as dog_walking.py . This is a little trickier.

Start by implementing a method just like a speak()method. As for the method in the Petsclass, you will need to iterate over the list of dogs and then call the method itself.

The output should look like this:

```
Tom is walking!
Fletcher is walking!
Larry is walking!
```

Solution: "dog walking"

```python
# Parent class
class Pets:

    dogs = []

    def __init__ (self, dogs):
        self.dogs = dogs

    def walk (self):
        for dog in self.dogs:
            print (dog.walk ())

# Parent class
class Dog:

    # Class attribute
    species = 'mammal'
    is_hungry = True

    # Initializer / instance attributes
    def __init__ (self, name, age):
        self.name = name
        self.age = age

    # Instance method
    def description (self):
        return self.name, self.age

    # Instance method
    def speak (self, sound):
        return "%s says %s" % (self.name, sound)

    # Instance method
    def eat (self):
        self.is_hungry = False
```

```
def walk (self):
    return "%s is walking!" % (self.name)


# Child class (inherits from Dog class)
class RussellTerrier (Dog):
    def run (self, speed):
        return "%s runs%s s" % (self.name, speed)


# Child class (inherits from Dog class)
class Bulldog (Dog):
    def run (self, speed):
        return "%s runs%s s" % (self.name, speed)

# Create instances of dogs
my_dogs = [
    Bulldog ("Tom", 6),
    RussellTerrier ("Fletcher", 7),
    Dog ("Larry", 9)
]

# Instantiate the Pet class
my_pets = Pets (my_dogs)

# Output
my_pets.walk ()
```

Exercise: "Testing Understanding"

Answer the following OOP questions to verify your learning progress:

1. What class?
2. What an example?
3. What is the relationship between class and instance?
4. What Python syntax is used to define a new class?
5. What is the spelling convention for a class name?
6. How do you create or create an instance of a class?
7. How do you access the attributes and behavior of an instance of a class?
8. What kind of method?
9. What is the purpose self?
10. What is the purpose of the init method?
11. Describe how inheritance helps prevent code duplication.
12. Can child classes override the properties of their parents?

Solution: "Test of understanding" Show hide

1. A class mechanism used to create new custom data structures. It contains data, as well as methods used to process this data.
2. An instance is a copy of a class with actual values, literally an object of a particular class.
3. While a class is a plan used to describe how to create something, instances are objects created from these drawings.
4. class PythonClassName:
5. Capitalized CamelCase designation - i.e. PythonClassName()
6. You use the class name followed by parentheses. So if the name of the class Dog(), the instance of the dog will be - my_class = Dog().
7. With dot notation - for example, instance_name.attribute_name
8. A function that defined inside a class.
9. The first argument of each method refers to the current instance of the class, which is called by the convention self. The init method self refers to a newly created object, while in other methods, it a self refers into the instance whose method was called. For more on the init con self, check out this article.
10. initThe method initializes an instance of the class.
11. Child classes inherit all the attributes and behavior of the parent.
12. Yes.

CONCLUSION

Now you should know what classes are, why you want or should use them, and how to create parent and child classes to better structure your programs.

Remember that OOP is a programming paradigm, not a Python concept. Most modern programming languages, such as Java, C #, C ++, follow the principles of OOP. So the good news is that learning the basics of object-oriented programming will be useful to you in a variety of circumstances - whether you work in Python or not.

Now the industry does not stand still and there are more and more web sites, services and companies that need specialists.

Demand for developers is growing, but competition among them is growing.

To be the best in your business, you need to be almost an absolutely universal person who can write a website, create a design for it, and promote it yourself.

In this regard, even a person who has never sat at this computer begins to think, but should I try?

But very often it turns out that such enthusiasts burn out at the initial stage, without having tried themselves in this matter.

Or maybe he would become a brilliant creator of code? Would create something new? This we will not know.

Every day, the threshold for entering programming is growing. You can never predict what new language will come out.

Such an abundance breaks all the desire of a newly minted programmer and he is lost in this ocean of information.

All these javascripts of yours ... pythons ... what fear ..

A great misconception is the obligation to know mathematics. Yes, it is needed, but only in a narrow field, but it is also useful for understanding some aspects.

The advice that can be given to people who are just starting their activity is not to chase everything at once. Allow yourself time to think.

What do I want to do? Create a program for everyone to be useful? Create additional services to simplify any tasks? Or do you really have to go make games?

The second advice will be to answer my question how much time am I ready to devote to this? The third point is to think about how fast you want to achieve your intended result.

So, there is no "easy way" to start programming, it all depends on you - your interest, what you want to do and your tasks.

In any case, you need to try and do everything possible in your power. Good luck in your endeavors!

www.ingramcontent.com/pod-product-compliance
Lightning Source LLC
La Vergne TN
LVHW051248050326
832903LV00028B/2639